CONTENTS

Introduction

The online edition of this book is at http://booksllc.net/?q=Category:Democratic% 5Feducation. It's hyperlinked and may be updated. Where we have recommended related pages, you can read them at http://booksllc.net/?q= followed by the page's title. Most entries in the book's index also have a dedicated page at http://booksllc.net/?q= followed by the index entry.

Each chapter in this book ends with a URL to a hyperlinked online version. Use the online version to access related pages, websites, footnote URLs. You can click the history tab on the online version to see a list of the chapter's contributors. While we have included photo captions in the book, due to copyright restrictions you can only view the photos online. You also need to go to the online edition to view some formula symbols.

The online version of this book is part of Wikipedia, a multilingual, web-based encyclopedia.

Wikipedia is written collaboratively. Since its creation in 2001, Wikipedia has grown rapidly into one of the largest reference web sites, attracting nearly 68 million visitors monthly. There are more than 91,000 active contributors working on more than 15 million articles in more than 270 languages. Every day, hundreds of thousands of active from around the world collectively make tens of thousands of edits and create thousands of new articles.

After a long process of discussion, debate, and argument, articles gradually take on a neutral point of view reached through consensus. Additional editors expand and contribute to articles and strive to achieve balance and comprehensive coverage. Wikipedia's intent is to cover existing knowledge which is verifiable from other sources. The ideal Wikipedia article is well-written, balanced, neutral, and encyclopedic, containing comprehensive, notable, verifiable knowledge.

Wikipedia is open to a large contributor base, drawing a large number of editors from diverse backgrounds. This allows Wikipedia to significantly reduce regional and cultural bias found in many other publications, and makes it very difficult for any group to censor and impose bias. A large, diverse editor base also provides access and breadth on subject matter that is otherwise inaccessible or little documented.

Think you can improve the book? If so, simply go to the online version and suggest changes. If accepted, your additions could appear in the next edition!

A. S. NEILL

Alexander Sutherland Neill

- o Neill on his birthday
- o Born: 17 October 1883 (1883-10-17) Forfar, Scotland
- o Died: 23 September 1973 (1973-09-24) (aged 89) Aldeburgh, Suffolk, England
- o Occupation: Educator, author
- o Known for: founding Summerhill School, advocacy of personal freedom for children, progressive education

Alexander Sutherland Neill (17 October 1883 - 23 September 1973) was a Scottish progressive educator, author and founder of Summerhill school, which remains open and continues to follow his educational philosophy to this day. He is best known as an advocate of personal freedom for children.

Personal background

Neill was born in Forfar, the son of a schoolteacher. After acting as a pupil-teacher for his father, he studied at the University of Edinburgh and obtained an M.A. degree in

1912. In 1914 he became headmaster of the Gretna Green School in Scotland. During this period, his growing discontent could be traced in notes which he later published. In these notes, he described himself as "just enough of a Nietzschian to protest against teaching children to be meek and lowly"[1] and wrote (in *A Dominie's Log*) that he was "trying to form minds that will question and destroy and rebuild".

Educational philosophy

Neill believed that the happiness of the child should be the paramount consideration in decisions about the child's upbringing, and that this happiness grew from a sense of personal freedom. He felt that deprivation of this sense of freedom during childhood, and the consequent unhappiness experienced by the repressed child, was responsible for many of the psychological disorders of adulthood.

The main focus of educational interest and research at that time was the question of how best to produce obedient soldiers who would uncritically follow orders in battle, so Neill's ideas, which tried to help children achieve self-determination and encouraged critical thinking rather than blind obedience, were seen as backward, radical, or at best, controversial.

Many of Neill's ideas are widely accepted today, although there are still many more "traditional" thinkers within the educational establishment who regard Neill's ideas as threatening the existing social order, and therefore controversial.

In 1921 Neill founded Summerhill School to demonstrate his educational theories in practice. These included a belief that children learn better when they are not compelled to attend lessons. The school is also managed democratically, with regular meetings to determine school rules. Pupils have equal voting rights with school staff.

Neill's Summerhill School experience demonstrated that, free from the coercion of traditional schools, students tended to respond by developing self-motivation, rather than self-indulgence. Externally imposed discipline, Neill felt, actually prevented internal, self-discipline from developing. He therefore considered that children who attended Summerhill were likely to emerge with better-developed critical thinking skills and greater self-discipline than children educated in compulsion-based schools.

These tendencies were perhaps all the more remarkable considering that the children accepted by Summerhill were often from problematic backgrounds, where parental conflict or neglect had resulted in children arriving in a particularly unhappy state of mind. The therapeutic value of Summerhill's environment was demonstrated by the improvement of many children who had been rejected by conventional schools, yet flourished at Summerhill.

Strongly influenced by the contemporary work of Sigmund Freud and Wilhelm Reich, Neill was opposed to sexual repression and the imposition of the strict Victorian values of his childhood era. He stated clearly that to be anti-sex was to be anti-life. Naturally, these views made him unpopular with many establishment figures of the time.

Life at Summerhill

As headmaster of Summerhill, Neill taught classes in Algebra, Geometry and Metalworking. He often said that he admired those who were skilled craftsmen more than those whose skills were purely intellectual. Neill held that because attendance was optional, the classes themselves could be more rigorous. Students learned more quickly, and more deeply, because they were learning by choice, not compulsion.

Neill also had special "private lessons" with pupils, which included discussions of personal issues and amounted to a form of psychotherapy. He later abandoned these "PLs", finding that children who did not have PLs were still cured of delinquent behaviour; he therefore concluded that freedom was the cure, not psychotherapy.

During his teaching career he wrote dozens of books, including the "Dominie" (Scottish word for teacher) series, beginning with *A Dominie's Log* (1916). His most influential book was *Summerhill: A Radical Approach to Child Rearing* (1960) which created a storm in U.S. educational circles. His last work was his autobiography, *Neill, Neill, Orange Peel!* (1973) He also wrote humorous books for children, like *The Last Man Alive* (1939).

A. S. Neill was married twice; his second wife Ena Wood Neill administered Summerhill school with him for many decades until their daughter, Zoe Redhead, took over the school as headmistress.

Influences on Neill's thought

Neill's biggest mentor in education was the British educator Homer Lane. Neill was also an admirer and close friend of psychoanalytical innovator Wilhelm Reich and a student of Freudian psychoanalysis, though in his autobiography he wrote that "Much of what I thought I had learned from the psychoanalysts has disappeared with time". [2]

Another major contributor to the field of Libertarian Education was Bertrand Russell whose own self-founded Beacon Hill School (England) (one of several schools bearing this name) is often compared with Summerhill. Russell was a correspondent of Neill and offered his support.

Criticisms of Neill

Many within the educational establishment felt threatened by Neill's work, and criticism of Neill was correspondingly harsh, and often inaccurate. Many published *ad hominem* attacks accusing Neill of various failings including naivety and unrealistic idealism, or even downright moral indifference. Neill was similarly criticized for bringing notions of Freudian repression into an educational setting.

Such critics often focused on what they (falsely) claimed to be the laxness of sexual morality at Summerhill.

Neill's educational legacy

Neill's notions of freedom and education, considered controversial in their time, influenced many of the progressive educators who came after him.

Modern advocates, such as John Taylor Gatto, John Holt and many others in the unschooling movement, democratic school movement, free school movement and homeschooling movements, have taken Neill's ideas further and updated them, providing energetic and radical critiques of the compulsion-based schooling which is still prevalent in most countries.

Due to the continuing international corporate demand for employees who can think critically and be self-motivated, as well as to the growing demand from parents for a system of education which reflects their ambitions for their children, compulsion-based systems in many countries are now gradually being reformed along much the same lines that Neill recommended.

Summerhill School, which Neill founded, has recently (2007) been accepted by the UK educational establishment, in particular OFSTED, as providing a good quality of academic education for children. Summerhill has also been recognised by the United Nations for its exceptionally good treatment of children.

"The convention of the Rights of the Child makes particular reference to children's rights to participate in decisions affecting them and Summerhill, through its very approach to education, embodies this right in a way that surpasses expectation." - Paulo David, Secretary, UN Committee on the Rights of the Child

Works

- *A Dominie s Log* (1915)
- *A Dominie Dismissed* (1916)
- *Booming of Bunkie* (1919)
- *Carroty Broon* (1920)
- *A Dominie in Doubt* (1920)
- *A Dominie Abroad* (1922)
- *A Dominie s Five* (1924)
- *The Problem Child* (1926)
- *The Problem Parent* (1932)
- *Is Scotland Educated?* (1936)
- *That Dreadful School* (1937)

o *The Last Man Alive* (1938)
o *The Problem Teacher* (1939)
o *Hearts Not Heads in the School* (1945)
o *The Problem Family* (1949)
o *The Free Child* (1953)
o *Summerhill: A Radical Approach to Child Rearing* (Preface by Erich Fromm) (1960)
o *Freedom, Not License!* (1966)
o *Talking of Summerhill* (1967)
o *Children's Rights: Toward the Liberation of the Child* (with Leila Berg, Paul Adams, Nan Berger, Michael Duane, and Robert Ollendorff) (1971)
o *Neill, Neill, Orange Peel!* (1972)

Published Correspondence

o *Record of a friendship: the correspondence between Wilhelm Reich and A. S. Neill, 1936-1957* (1982)
o *All the Best, Neill: Letters from Summerhill* (1984)

Portrait bust of A.S. Neill

A.S. Neill sat for sculptor Alan Thornhill for a portrait[3] in clay. The correspondence file relating to the A.S. Neill portrait sculpture is held in the archive[4] of the Henry Moore Foundation's Henry Moore Institute in Leeds and the terracotta remains in the collection of the artist. Bronzes are in the public collections of The College of Orgonomy[5], New York and the Scottish National Portrait Gallery, Edinburgh (collection reference PG2204).

References (URLs online)

o 1. Neill, A.S. (1915). A Dominie's Log. READ BOOKS, 2007 Page 66. ISBN 1406763535, 9781406763539
o 2. Neill, A.S. (1973). *Neill! Neill! Orange Peel!*. Weidenfeld and Nicolson. pp. 163. ISBN 0-297-76554X.
o 3. portrait head of A.S.Neill image of sculpture
o 4.   http://www.henry-moore-fdn.co.uk/matrix_engine/content.php?page_id=584 HMI Archive
o 5. The American College of Orgonomy

o Neill, Alexander S.: *Summerhill School - A New View of Childhood*. New York: St. Martin's Griffin, 1996 ISBN 0-312-14137-8.
o Croall, Jonathan: *Neill of Summerhill - The Permanent Rebel*. London: Routledge & Kegan Paul, 1983 ISBN 0-7100-9300-4
o Croall, Jonathan (ed): *All the Best, Neill. Letters from Summerhill*. London: André Deutsch, 1983 ISBN 0-233-97594-2 (A collection of letters by Neill to people like H.G. Wells, Bertrand Russell, Henry Miller, Wilhelm Reich, Paul Goodman, Homer Lane, and others)

o Walmsley, John. *Neill & Summerhill: A pictorial study.* Baltimore: Penguin, 1969 ISBN 0-14-080134-0
o Sims, Hylda: *Inspecting the island.* Ipswich (UK): Seven Ply Yarns, 2000 ISBN 0-9538797-0-4 (A novel by an ex-Summerhill pupil)
o Vaughan, Mark (ed) with contributions from A. S. Neill, Zoe Neill Readhead, Tim Brighouse and Ian Stronach: "Summerhill and A. S. Neill". Maidenhead: Open University Press, McGraw-Hill Education, 2004 ISBN 0-335-21913-6.

Websites (URLs online)

o Summerhill School
o Page of Summerhill and A. S. Neill (German)
o A.S. Neill on Project Gutenberg
o ALEXANDER SUTHERLAND NEILL (1883 1973) (PDF), by Jean-François Saffange, originally published in vol. XXIV, no. 1/2, 1994 of UNESCO's Prospects:the quarterly review of comparative education

A hyperlinked version of this chapter is at http://booksllc.net?q=A%2E%5FS%2E% 5FNeill

2

ALBANY FREE SCHOOL

The **Free School (Albany)** is a day school for 60 students aged two to fourteen founded in 1969 by Mary Leue. The student population is as diverse as the surrounding racially and socioeconomically mixed downtown neighborhood, with approximately half of the kids coming from the inner city, one-fourth from uptown, and the remainder from outlying areas. The school operates with a sliding scale tuition and no one is turned away for financial reasons.

Their educational philosophy is based on the belief that learning is an instinctive act in which children engage joyfully and of their own accord when they are allowed to follow their own rhythms and interests. They also believe that all children possess a unique set of gifts that must be allowed to develop according to each child s own inner timetable. Therefore there are no compulsory classes, grades or standardized tests. Formal student assessment takes place at mid-year when teachers collaborate on a narrative report about each student s growth and development followed by an in-depth parent conference. The school is governed democratically through a weekly all-school meeting. Conflicts and other urgent problems are addressed on an ad hoc basis in student-led council meetings that can be called at any time.

The Free School claims to be a community in which emotional, personal and social needs are given as much attention as academic ones, and the essential ingredients of a life well lived are the highest concern of all.

Professional Memberships & Affiliations:

Member School:

- Northeast Association of Independent Democratic Schools (NAIDS)
- Alternative Education Resource Organization (AERO)
- International Democratic Education Network (IDEN)

Participating School:

- International Democratic Education Conference (IDEC)

Websites (URLs online)

- The Free School's website - www.albanyfreeschool.com
- Harriet Tubman Free School

Coordinates: 42°38 44 N 73°45 28 W / 42.64561°N 73.75779°W / 42.64561; - 73.75779

A hyperlinked version of this chapter is at http://booksllc.net?q=Albany%5FFree% 5FSchool

3

ANTIOCH COLLEGE

Antioch College

- o Motto: *Be ashamed to die until you have won some victory for humanity.*
- o Established: 1853
- o Type: Private undergraduate
- o Endowment: $36.2 million[1]
- o Location: Yellow Springs, Ohio, United States
- o Website: http://antiochcollege.org/

Online image: The distinctive towers of Antioch's Main Building

Antioch College was a private, independent liberal arts college in Yellow Springs, Ohio. It was the founder and the flagship institution of the six-campus Antioch University system. Founded in 1852 by the Christian Connection, the college began operating in 1853 with the distinguished scholar Horace Mann as its first president. The college's educational approach blended practical work experience with classroom learning, and participatory community governance. Students received narrative evaluations instead of academic letter grades. The college's enrollment during the last academic year that it was open for classes (2007-08) was fewer than 200 students.[2]

In June 2007, the University s Board of Trustees announced that Antioch College would be suspending operations as of July 2008, with an attempted re-opening in 2012.[3] On June 30, 2009, it was announced that Antioch University had agreed to transfer its campus, its endowment, and the adjoining Glen Helen Nature Preserve to the Antioch College Continuation Corporation (ACCC), an alumni-led group seeking to find a way to re-open the college. The transfer of assets was completed on September 4, 2009. Over half of the Antioch College faculty had filed a lawsuit in August 2007 to bar Antioch University from discharging the college's tenured faculty members, or liquidating the college's financial assets.[4] This legal case was dismissed by the Greene County Common Pleas Court on November 26, 2008. The Court held that "the decision to declare financial exigency, or to use less drastic means than that, to alleviate the University's financial problems is a business judgment." [5] The announcement of the suspension of the College's operations sparked an intensive fundraising drive by the college's alumni association.[6] On November 3, 2007, the University Board of Trustees agreed to explore alternatives for the college to remain open.[7] Negotiations broke down in late March 2008, however, greatly increasing the likelihood that the college would close at the end of the 2007-2008 academic year.[8]

Antioch College closed in June 2008. However, the trustees passed a resolution on June 7, 2008, stating "that the Trustees request the [Alumni] Association create the necessary process, plans, and resources for the development of an independent four-year, residential, liberal arts college in Yellow Springs, Ohio, and a business plan for the transfer of assets from the University, and to present those plans to the Trustees for their consideration and approval and that the Association present its timetable for implementing this request to the Trustees." On July 18, 2008, the Dayton Daily News reported that the directors of the Antioch College Alumni Association and the trustees of Antioch University had "agreed on the framework for a plan to create a new, fully independent Antioch College."[9]

Antioch College is a member of the Great Lakes Colleges Association, which mediated negotiations for transfer of the College from Antioch University to the ACCC, and the North American Alliance for Green Education. It was also formerly a member of the Eco League. Current efforts to keep the College alive include the Nonstop Liberal Arts Institute and the College Revival Fund [10]. On July 17, 2008, the Antioch University Board of Trustees and the Board of Directors of the Antioch College Alumni Association announced their intention to create a fully independent Antioch College that would open at an early date. The negotiations will be facilitated in part by the Great Lakes College Association. [11].

History

On October 5, 1850, the General Convention of the Christian Church passed a resolution stating "that our responsibility to the community, and the advancement of our interests as a denomination, demand of us the establishing of a College." The delegates further pledged "the sum of one hundred thousand dollars as the standard by which to measure our zeal and our effort in raising the means for establishing the contemplated College." The Committee on the Plan for a College was formed to undertake the founding of a college, and make decisions regarding the name of the school, the endowment, fundraising, faculty, and administration.[12] Most notably, the committee decided that the college "shall afford equal privileges to students of both sexes."[13] The Christian Connection sect wanted the new college to be sectarian, but the planning committee decided otherwise.

Despite its enthusiasm, the Christian Connection's fundraising efforts proved insufficient. The money raised before the school opened failed to cover even the cost of the three original buildings, much less create an endowment.[14] The Unitarian Church contributed an equal amount of funds and nearly as many students to the new school, causing denominational strife early on.[14]

Early years

Horace Mann, Antioch's first president, ran the college from its founding in 1853 until his death in 1859. The young college had relatively high academic standards, and "good moral character" was a requirement for graduation.[15] The first curriculum focused on Latin, Greek, mathematics, history, philosophy and science, and offered electives in art, botany, pedagogy, and modern languages.[16] Tuition was $24 a year, and the first graduating class consisted of 28 students. Although the founders planned for approximately 1,000 students, enrollment only exceeded 500 once in the 19th century, in 1857.[17]

Online image: Horace Mann, Antioch's first president.

One notable character in Antioch's history is Rebecca Pennell, who was one of the college's ten original faculty members. She was the first female college professor in the United States to have the same rank and pay as her male colleagues.[18] Her home, now part of the Antioch campus and called Pennell House, served in recent years as community space for several of Antioch's student-led independent groups.

In 1859, Mann gave his final commencement speech, including what became the college's motto: "Be ashamed to die until you have won some victory for humanity."[19] Mann died in August and was initially interred on the Antioch College grounds. The next year, he was reinterred in Providence, Rhode Island, next to his first wife.

The original founders gave no consideration to the question of whether Antioch should admit students of color, neither forbidding nor explicitly allowing it.[20] The associated preparatory school admitted two African American girls during the mid-

1850s, an action one trustee responded to by resigning and removing his own children from the school. His opinion was apparently the minority one, though, as the African American students were not withdrawn.[21] In 1863, Antioch trustee John Phillips proposed a resolution stating "the Trustees of Antioch College cannot, according to the Charter, reject persons on account of color." The resolution passed with nine trustees in favor and four opposed. However, the college remained nearly all white until after World War II, when the school undertook a minority recruitment program.

Antioch College faced financial difficulties in its first years, mostly due to the Panic of 1857.[22] From 1857 to 1859, Antioch ran an annual deficit of US$5,000, out of a total budget of US$13,000.[23] In 1858, Antioch was bankrupt. Mann died in 1859 and the college was reorganized, but deficits continued.[23] Mann's successor, Thomas Hill, took Antioch's presidency on the condition that faculty salaries be paid despite deficits. Despite this stipulation, his salary was often not paid, and he supported his family with loans. Hill and a colleague attempted to raise an endowment, but potential donors were put off by the strong sectarian leanings of some of the college's trustees.[24] Hill resigned in 1862 due to increasing financial troubles, sectarian conflict between Christian Connection and Unitarian trustees, and his election as president of Harvard. In 1862, the college was closed until finances improved and remained closed until after the end of the Civil War.

In 1865, the college reopened, now administered by the Unitarian Church. The financial health of the college seemed improved, as the Unitarians had raised a US$100,000 endowment in the space of two months.[25] The endowment was originally invested in government bonds and later in real estate and timber. The investment income, while performing well, was still insufficient to maintain the college at the high level desired by the trustees. Some of the principal was lost to foreclosures during the Long Depression, which began in 1873.[25] The college closed again from 1881 1882 to allow the endowment to recover.

In 1869, when the Cincinnati Red Stockings began their inaugural season as history's first professional baseball team, they played a preseason game at the site of what is now the Grand Union Terminal in Cincinnati against the Antiochs, who were regarded as one of the finest amateur clubs in Ohio. The game was played on May 15, 1869, and Cincinnati defeated Antioch 41-7. Antioch had been scheduled to host the first game of this professional tour on May 31, 1869, but pouring rain and an unplayable field kept the Red Stockings inside the Yellow Springs House until they left for Mansfield. So, while Antioch was not a part of the first professional baseball game, the college does hold claim to hosting the first ever rainout in professional baseball.[26]

1900-1945

The turn of the century saw little improvement in the college's finances. In 1900 faculty made between US$500 and $700 a year, very low for the time, and the president was paid $1,500 a year. In contrast, Horace Mann's annual salary had been $3,000 more than forty years prior.[27] Enrollment did increase significantly under the presidency of Simeon D. Fess, who served from 1906 to 1917. In 1912 he was elected to the United States House of Representatives, and served three of his five total terms while also acting as president of Antioch.

World War I had little effect, good or bad, on the college and though some people contracted influenza during the Spanish flu epidemic, there were no deaths.[28] In February 1919, the Young Men's Christian Association attempted a peaceful takeover of the college, offering to raise an endowment of US$500,000 if Antioch would serve as the official national college of the YMCA. The YMCA proposal was received positively by the college's trustees and enacted by a unanimous vote, and Grant Perkins, a YMCA executive, assumed the college's presidency. By May, Perkins had resigned, reporting that he was not prepared to raise the necessary funds.[28]

In June 1919, several candidates were submitted to the trustees, including Arthur Morgan. Morgan was elected to the board without any prior notification of his candidacy. An engineer, he had been involved in planning a college in upstate New York that would have included work-study along with a more traditional curriculum. Morgan presented his plan for "practical industrial education" to the trustees, which accepted the new plan. Antioch closed for a third time while the curriculum was reorganized and the co-op program developed. In 1920, Morgan was unanimously elected president and, in 1921, the college reopened with the cooperative education program.[29]

Online image: Arthur E. Morgan, circa 1921.

The early co-op program was not required; students could enter as traditional students or cooperative education students. Despite this, by the 1935 academic year, nearly 80% of the student body had chosen the cooperative program. Students initially studied for eight-week-long terms alternating with eight-week-long work experiences. Male students generally took apprenticeships with craftsmen or jobs in factories; female students often served as nursing or teaching assistants. In 1921, when the program was inaugurated, fewer than 1% of available co-op jobs were located outside of Ohio, but this had grown to about 75% within 15 years.[30]

The college had no black students from 1899 1929 and only two from 1929 1936 (neither graduated), so it is unknown how racial discrimination among employers affected the co-op program. While Antioch itself had no religious quotas (elsewhere common until the 1940s), many employers discriminated against Jews, a fact that limited the number of Jewish students at Antioch. The program suffered for available positions during the Great Depression, prompting the college to employ many students at industrial jobs on campus.[30]

In 1926, the college's Administrative Council was formed as an advisory body to the president. It was chartered in 1930. The Administrative Council was originally a faculty-only body, though a student seat was added in 1941. Over time, the Administrative Council became the primary policy-making body of the College. The Community Council was established a short time later, to advise on and manage what at other college campuses would be considered "student concerns". At Antioch, these matters, such as campus artistic and cultural life, have been regarded as community-wide issues, affecting students, staff, faculty members and administrators.

1945-2000

Beginning in the 1940s, Antioch was considered an early bastion of student activism, anti-racism, and progressive thought. During World War II, Antioch, among other eastern colleges, with the help of Victor Goertzel, participated in a program which arranged for students of Japanese origin interned in Relocation camps to enroll in college. In 1943 the college Race Relations Committee began offering scholarships to non-white students to help diversify the campus, which had been mostly white since its founding. The first scholarship recipient was Edythe Scott, elder sister of Coretta Scott King. Coretta Scott received the scholarship and attended Antioch two years after her sister.[31] Antioch was one of the first historically white colleges to actively recruit black students. Antioch was also the first historically white college to appoint a black person to be chair of an academic department, when Walter Anderson was appointed chair of the music department.

In the 1950s Antioch faced pressure from the powerful House Un-American Activities Committee and faced criticism from many area newspapers because it did not expel students and faculty accused of having Communist leanings. College officials stood firm, insisting that freedom begins not in suppressing unpopular ideas but in holding all ideas up to the light. The school, including professors and administration, was also involved in the early stages of the American Civil Rights Movement and was a supporter of free speech.

In 1965, Dr. Martin Luther King Jr. gave the commencement speech.

Antioch became increasingly progressive and financially healthy during the 1960s and early 1970s under the Presidency of Dr. James P. Dixon. The student body topped out at around 2,400 students, the college owned property all over Yellow Springs and beyond, and the college grew throughout the decade. It began to appear in literary works and other media as an icon of youth culture, serving, for example, as the setting for a portion of Philip Roth's most popular novel, "Portnoy's Complaint". At this time, Antioch became one of the primary sources of student radicalism, the New Left, the anti-Vietnam War movement, and the Black Power movement in the region. The town of Yellow Springs became an island of liberal and progressive activism in southern Ohio, an otherwise very politically conservative region.

In many instances, the environment of the school spurred its students to activism. Eleanor Holmes Norton, future congressional delegate for Washington, D.C., recalled her time at Antioch as one "when the first real action that could be called movement action was ignited", according to an interview now available in the National Security Archives.[32]

The 1970s saw the college continue to develop its reputation as a source of activism and progressive political thought. Several graduate satellite schools around the country, under the Antioch University name (with the college as a base), were established as well, including the McGregor School (now known as Antioch University McGregor located on a new campus in Yellow Springs that opened September 2007). Antioch University New England was the first graduate school offshoot in 1964. The university campuses are located in Keene, New Hampshire; Seattle, Washington; Los Angeles, California; and Santa Barbara, California. The corporation of Antioch College legally changed its name to Antioch University in 1978. The name Antioch College continued to be used for the residential undergraduate program in Yellow Springs, OH.

Funding and enrollment at the college began to decline as the University system was created. In the late 1970s, the new Antioch University system partially collapsed, leaving Antioch College in dire financial straits by the beginning of the 1980s. Beginning in the mid 1980s and continuing through the 1990s, under the leadership of Antioch Presidents Alan Guskin and Bob Devine, Antioch's enrollment figures and financial health improved, though college enrollment never surpassed 1,000 students. The campus underwent renovations and many buildings that had been boarded up were repaired and reopened, including South Hall, one of the college's three original buildings.

The Sexual Offense Prevention Policy

In 1993 Antioch became the focus of national attention with its "Sexual Offense Prevention Policy." Under this policy, consent for sexual behavior must be "(a) verbal, (b) mutual, and (c) reiterated for every new level of sexual behavior." [33] This policy was initiated after two date rapes reportedly occurred on the Antioch College campus during the 1990-91 academic year. A group of students formed under the name "Womyn of Antioch" to address their concern that sexual offenses in general were not being taken seriously enough by the administration or some in the campus community.[34] Advocates of the policy explain that the original "Sexual Offense Policy," as it was then called, was created during a couple of late-night meetings in the campus Womyn's Center, and that "this original policy was questionable. It was not legally binding, no rights were given to the accused, and it called for immediate expulsion of the accused with no formal process."[34] The policy, both as it then stood and as revised, uniquely viewed any sexual offense as not simply a violation of the victim's rights, but as an offense against the entire campus community. It was revised to focus more on education and less on punishment and clarified in a series of community meetings during the 1991-92 academic year. Once revised, it was endorsed by the entire campus and the Board of Trustees, and thus became the official policy of the college that year.

This revised policy attracted renewed national publicity two years later, during the fall semester of the 1993-94 academic year, allegedly when a student doing a co-op on the west coast mentioned the policy to a California campus newspaper reporter. An Associated Press reporter picked up the story in the early days of the term,[35] and a media frenzy ensued, one that arguably garnered more attention to Antioch than anything since the student strike of 1973. The policy was often ridiculed by the mainstream American news media that fall, even becoming the butt of a Saturday Night Live sketch, entitled "Is It Date Rape?" Some media outlets voiced support for the policy. For example, syndicated columnist Ellen Goodman asserted that most "sexual policy makers write like lawyers in love," and that, likewise, "at Antioch the authors could use some poetry, and passion." But, she was ultimately sympathetic to their goals of leveling the sexual playing field and making students think about what consent means, saying that the Antioch campus "has the plot line just about right."[36]

The 21st century

In 2000, Antioch College was again subject to media attention after inviting political activist and death row inmate Mumia Abu Jamal and transgendered rights advocate and Jamal supporter Leslie Feinberg to be commencement speakers. Graduating students had chosen Jamal and Feinberg to highlight their concerns with capital punishment and the American criminal justice system. Many conservative commentators criticized the Antioch administration for allowing students to choose such controversial commencement speakers and the college administration received death threats. Antioch President Bob Devine chose not to overturn the students' choice of speakers, citing the ideals of free speech and free exchange of ideas, and likened the media reaction to the coverage of Martin Luther King, Jr.'s 1965 commencement address.[37]

In the early 2000s enrollment declined to just over 600 students. This combined with a declining economy caused Antioch University to institute a "Renewal Plan" in 2003. The controversial plan called for restructuring Antioch's first year program into learning communities and upgrading campus facilities. Many students and faculty stated that they were shut out of planning. Antioch University's Board of Trustees committed to five years of funding for the renewal plan but discontinued this commitment to the college three years into the plan.[38]

Simultaneously with the announcement of the renewal plan, the University's Board of Trustees announced mandated staff cuts at the college, including the elimination of the Office of Multicultural Affairs. Student anger over the mandated renewal plan and program cuts led to a student-initiated protest entitled "People of Color Takeover", which garnered negative media attention. Partially in response to this, Antioch College created the Coretta Scott King Center for Cultural and Intellectual Freedom in 2006.[39]

With the implementation of the controversial renewal plan, enrollment dropped from 650 students to 370 in two years, a decline that many feel was a result of the curriculum change mandated by the Board of Trustees. At an Antioch University Board of Trustees meeting in June 2007 the Board stated that while the college was only in its third year of implementation of the plan they had not raised the funds needed, and that the college would be indefinitely closed at the end of the 2007-08 academic year.[38][40]

Many Antioch alumni and faculty, upset at the prospect of the loss of the college's legacy, began organizing and raising funds in an effort to save the college, keep it open without interruption, and gain greater transparency in its governance. In August 2007, the college faculty filed suit against the Board of Trustees, charging that the Board was violating various contractual obligations.[41]

Following a meeting between university and alumni representatives in August 2007, the Board of Trustees approved a resolution giving the Alumni Board until the October 2007 trustees' meeting to demonstrate the viability of an Alumni Board proposal to maintain the operations of the College.[42] Despite initially stating he would remain until December, Antioch president Steve Lawry abruptly stepped down as president on September 1, 2007. The role of president was turned over to a three-person group, comprising the Dean of Faculty, Director of Student Services, and Director of Communications.[43] While no reason for Lawry's immediate departure was given, it has been reported that he was forcibly ousted by the Board of Trustees.[44] In response to this reported ousting, the faculty gave Antioch University Chancellor Toni Murdock a vote of no confidence.[45]

A story about Antioch's closing in *The Chronicle of Higher Education* detailed the uncertain future of some faculty and staff members, along with the town of Yellow Springs, following suspended operations at the college. One professor, who got tenure 28 hours before the college announced its closing, had turned down other jobs in academia to work at Antioch. The story includes a slideshow showing outdated and crumbling buildings on campus.[46]

On November 3, 2007, the University Board of Trustees agreed to lift the suspension of the college, which would have seen the college operate continuously rather than closing. The Alumni Board embarked on a $100 million fundraising drive to build the college's endowment, raising more than $18 million in gifts and pledges by November 2007[7]. However, major donors balked out of concern that the deal did not make the college sufficiently autonomous from the university[47], and a group began meeting directly with the university, incorporating as the Antioch College Continuation Corporation (ACCC). On February 22, 2008 the university issued a press release reinstating the suspension, despite ongoing negotiations with the group.[48] On March 28, 2008, university trustees rejected a $12.2 million offer from the ACCC[49], which then offered $10 million for 10 seats on the 19-member board. On May 8, 2008, university trustees rejected the ACCC's "best and final" offer – $9.5 million for the college and another $6 million for the graduate campuses in exchange for eight board seats, with an additional four new trustees to be jointly agreed upon by the ACCC and current trustees[50].

The college closed as promised on June 30, 2008.

Continuation of Antioch College

The suspension of operations of the College led to an historic and unprecedented collaboration between the University and its College alumni association to explore a means to separate the College from the University in a manner which preserved the viability of both. The closure of Antioch College also spurred the creation of the Nonstop Liberal Arts Institute. Led by former faculty, staff, and students, and with the support of Yellow Springs residents, Nonstop aims to keep the values and mission of the College alive in the midst of its suspension [51]. Recognizing that any reopening of the College required the cooperation and substantial financial support of alumni, the Board of Governors of Antioch University adopted a resolution on June 8, 2008 requesting that the Alumni Association prepare a plan to bring the College back to vigor and vitality. Thereafter, the Antioch University Board of Governors and the Board of Directors of the Antioch College Alumni Association publicly announced on July 17, 2008 the creation of a new task force composed of University and Alumni representatives to develop a plan to create an independent Antioch College. The Alumni Association then delegated its role in the discussions to a limited group of alumni who had incorporated as Antioch College Continuation Corporation ("ACCC"), an Ohio non-profit corporation. The task force discussions were facilitated in part by the Great Lakes College Association. As the result of those discussions, ACCC and [11]. Antioch University agreed to an asset purchase agreement on June 30, 2009. That agreement called for the transfer of the College campus and the College endowment to ACCC which would operate the College as an independent corporation with its own fiduciary board of trustees. As part of the transaction, Antioch University licensed to ACCC an exclusive right to use the name "Antioch College". The parties closed on the transfer of assets on September 4, 2009, but any reopening of Antioch College is at least two years away.(reference Associated Press)

Profiles, recognition, and criticism

The *U.S. News & World Report* college and university rankings classify Antioch College as a third-tier Liberal Arts College.[52]

Antioch has been regularly included in the guidebook "Colleges That Change Lives" which declares that "there is no college or university in the country that makes a more profound difference in a young person's life or that creates more effective adults."[53]

Less positive opinions include that of George Will, who wrote in response to the college's announced closure that there is "a minuscule market for what Antioch sells for a tuition, room and board of $35,221 repressive liberalism unleavened by learning."[54]

During her remarks to the college in 2004 alumna Coretta Scott King stated that "Antioch students learn that it s not enough to have a great career, material wealth and a fulfilling family life. We are also called to serve, to share, to give and to do what we can to lift up the lives of others. No other college emphasizes this challenge so strongly. That s what makes Antioch so special."[55]

The Twilight Zone TV series includes an episode titled "The Changing of the Guard" that is considered to be "the Antioch episode" for its references to Antioch that include mention of Horace Mann and the school motto.

Noteworthy alumni

Business

- Theodore Levitt (1949), Economist

Edward E. Booher (1934), Publisher, President, McGraw Hill Book Co.

Education

- Warren Bennis (1951), Distinguished Professor of Business Administration at the University of Southern California, Chair of the Advisory Board of the Harvard University Kennedy School's Center for Public Leadership, author of more than thirty books on leadership
- Deborah Meier (1954), Educator, considered the founder of the modern small schools movement
- Myron D. Stewart (1973), District of Columbia Public School advocate and educator.
- Lisa Delpit (1974), author of *Other People's Children*, director of the Center for Urban Educational Excellence

Entertainment

- Peggy Ahwesh (1978), filmmaker & video artist
- John Flansburgh (1983), singer/songwriter, They Might Be Giants
- Herb Gardner (1958), playwright
- Ken Jenkins, actor, Dr. Bob Kelso on Scrubs (TV Series)
- Nick Katzman, blues musician
- John Korty (195?), TV and screenwriter [Emmy for "The Autobiography of Miss Jane Pittman", Oscar for documentary of Japanese Internment Camps]
- Peter Kurland, Academy Award-nominated sound mixer
- Nicholas Noxon (195?) Cinematographer and producer for National Geographic TV series
- Cliff Robertson (1946), Academy Award-winning actor
- Rod Serling (1950), the creator of *The Twilight Zone* TV series
- Mia Zapata (1989), lead singer of The Gits

Government

- Chester G. Atkins (1970), former United States Representative
- Bill Bradbury (1960), Oregon Secretary of State
- John de Jongh, United States Virgin Islands Governor
- Hattie N. Harrison, member of the Maryland House of Delegates
- A. Leon Higginbotham, Jr., civil rights advocate, author, United States federal judge
- Eleanor Holmes Norton (1960) Congressional Delegate, representing the District of Columbia
- Americus V. Rice Civil War general, U.S. Representative
- E. Denise Simmons, mayor of Cambridge, Massachusetts, and the first openly lesbian African-American Mayor of an American city

Military

- Marion Ross (1864), Civil War hero, Medal of Honor recipient

Science

- Mario Capecchi (B.S. 1961), co-recipient of the Nobel Prize in Physiology or Medicine in 2007
- Don Clark (1953), clinical psychologist, author
- Leland C. Clark, Jr. (B.S. 1941), biochemist and inventor
- Clifford Geertz (1950), anthropologist
- Stephen Jay Gould (1963), biologist, author
- Frances Degan Horowitz, educator and developmental psychologist
- Allan Pred (1957), geographer
- Joan Steitz (1963), molecular biologist and Sterling Professor at Yale University
- Judith G. Voet, B.S. - professor of chemistry and biochemistry at Swarthmore College and author of several widely-used biochemistry textbooks

Writers

- Lawrence Block (1960), author
- James Galvin (1974) poet/author
- David A. Horowitz, historian and author
- Peter Irons (1966), legal historian and author
- Laurence Leamer (1964)
- Franz Lidz (1973), journalist and author whose memoir, Unstrung Heroes, became a 1995 feature film directed by Diane Keaton
- Sylvia Nasar (1970), author, *A Beautiful Mind*
- Cary Nelson (1967), higher education activist, author
- Mark Strand (1957), poet
- Karl Grossman(1964), journalist and author
- John Robbins (1976), author of *Diet for a New America*, pioneer environmentalist, and veganism advocate

Others

- Olympia Brown (1860), suffragist, women's rights activist, minister

- Leo Drey (1939), conservationist
- Coretta Scott King (1951), human rights activist
- Robert Manry (1949), nautical explorer
- Gene Klotz (1957), Mathematician, educator, general baller.
- Luke Campbell Brennan 1985, Political Conspirator, Captain Chode.

References (URLs online)

- 1. Fain, Paul (2007-06-22). "Antioch's Closure Signals the End of an Era". The Chronicle of Higher Education.
- 2. Cohen, Patricia (April 20, 2008). "The College That Would Not Go Gently". *Education Life* (The New York Times). Retrieved 2008-04-22.
- 3. "Antioch College Suspends Operations to Design 21st Century Campus: State-of-the-Art Campus projected to open in 2012". Antioch College. 2007-06-12. Retrieved 2007-06-12.
- 4. Shapiro, Gary (2007-08-16). "Antioch College Faculty Revolts Against Proposed Closing of School". The New York Sun. Retrieved 2007-07-16.
- 5. *Townsend et al. v. Antioch University*, Case No. 2008-cv-0300, Greene County Common Pleas Court
- 6. "Alumni Resolution". Antioch College Alumni Board. 2007-06-24. Retrieved 2007-06-24.
- 7. Antioch College (November 3, 2007). ""Alumni Board and Board of Trustees Reach Unprecedented Agreement: Antioch College to Remain Open"". Press release. Retrieved 2007-11-04.
- 8. Chiddister, Diane (April 3, 2008). "Negotiations Between ACCC and University Come to a Halt". Yellow Springs News. Retrieved 2008-04-16.
- 9. Larsen, Dave (2008-07-18). "Task force formed to establish new Antioch College". Dayton Daily News. Retrieved 2008-07-18.
- 10. Kaiser, Rowan (2008-06-20). "The Story of Nonstop". The Record. Retrieved 2008-07-16.
- 11. White, Charla (2008-07-17). "Antioch College Alumni Association Creates Framework for Plan to Open Independent Antioch College with Support from Antioch University Board of Trustees" (PDF). Great Lakes College Association. Retrieved 2008-07-17.
- 12. Allen, Ira W. (1858). *History of the Rise, Difficulties & Suspension of Antioch College*. Columbus, Ohio: John Geary & Son. pp. 1.
- 13. Morgan, Joyce Elder (1938). *Horace Mann at Antioch*. Washington, D.C.: The Horace Mann Centennial Fund, National Education Association. pp. 150.
- 14. Straker, Robert L. (1954). *Brief Sketch of Antioch College (1853-1921)*. Yellow Springs, Ohio: Antioch College. pp. 4.
- 15. Morgan, Joyce Elder (1938). *Horace Mann at Antioch*. Washington, D.C.: The Horace Mann Centennial Fund, National Education Association. pp. 93.
- 16. Straker, Robert L. (1854). *Brief Sketch of Antioch (1853-1921)*. Yellow Springs, Ohio: Antioch College. pp. 6.
- 17. Morgan, Joyce Elmer (1938). *Horace Mann at Antioch*. Washington, D.C.: Horace Mann Centennial Fund, National Education Association. pp. 71.
- 18. Morgan, Joyce Elder (1938). *Horace Mann at Antioch*. Washington D.C.: The Horace Mann Centennial Fund, National Education Association. pp. 77.
- 19. Mann, Horace (June 29, 1859). *Baccalaureate Address of 1859*.

o 20. Straker, Robert L. (1954). *Brief Sketch of Antioch (1853-1921)*. Yellow Springs, Ohio: Antioch College. pp. 5.

o 21. Straker, Robert L. (1954). *Brief Sketch of Antioch College (1853-1921)*. Yellow Springs, Ohio: Antioch College. pp. 12.

o 22. Morgan, Joyce Elmer (1938). *Horace Mann at Antioch*. Washington D.C.: The Horace Mann Centennial Fund, National Education Association. pp. 74.

o 23. Straker, Robert L. (1954). *Brief Sketch of Antioch College (1853-1921)*. Yellow Springs, Ohio: Antioch College. pp. 8.

o 24. Straker, Robert L. (1954). *Brief Sketch of Antioch College (1853-1921)*. Yellow Springs, Ohio: Antioch College. pp. 9.

o 25. Straker, Robert L. (1954). *Brief Sketch of Antioch College (1853-1921)*. Yellow Springs, Ohio: Antioch College. pp. 13.

o 26. Guschov, Stephen D.. *The Red Stockings of Cincinnati: Base Ball's First All-Professional Team and its Historic 1869 and 1870 Seasons*. Jefferson, N.C.: McFarland & Co., 1998. ISBN 0786404671. Page 45. For more information about the rainout, see also two entries from "The Annotated This Day in Baseball History" blog: [1] [2]

o 27. Straker, Robert L. (1954). *Brief Sketch of Antioch College*. Yellow Springs, Ohio: Antioch College. pp. 19.

o 28. Straker, Robert L. (1954). *Brief Sketch of Antioch College*. Yellow Springs, Ohio: Antioch College. pp. 21.

o 29. Straker, Robert L. (1954). *Brief Sketch of Antioch College*. Yellow Springs, Ohio: Antioch College. pp. 22.

o 30. Morgan, Joyce elder (1938). *Horace Mann at Antioch*. Washington, D.C.: The Horace Mann Centennial Fund, National Education Association. pp. 157 158.

o 31. Scott, Coretta (April-June, 1922). "Why I Came to College" (Scholar search). *Opportunity, Journal of Negro Life* **26** (2). Retrieved 2007-06-25.

o 32. Holmes Norton, Eleanor (1996-07-11). "National Security Archive Interview". The National Security Archives at George Washington University. Retrieved 2007-06-25.

o 33. Burrow, Jason J.; Hannon, Roseann; Hall, David (15 September 1998). "College Students' Perceptions of Women's Verbal and Nonverbal Consent for Sexual Intercourse". *Electronic Journal of Human Sexuality* **1**.

o 34. "Antioch College Sexual Offense Prevention Policy, Addendum A". Antioch College. Retrieved 2007-07-21.

o 35. "Sex Consent Policy Set at Antioch". Columbus Dispatch. pp. 4D.

o 36. Goodman, Ellen (1993-09-19). "The struggle on college campuses to create a standard of sexual equality". The Boston Globe. pp. 75.

o 37. "Commencement 2000: The Keynote Speakers" (PDF). The Antioch Record. 2000-04-29. pp. 1. Retrieved 2007-07-15.

o 38. Lawry, Steve (2007-06-22). "State of the College Address". Retrieved 2007-06-23.

o 39. "About the Center". The Coretta Scott King Center for Cultural and Intellectual Freedom. Retrieved 2007-09-04.

o 40. Fain, Paul (June 13, 2007). "Antioch College to Close; Board Hopes to Reopen in 2012". *The Chronicle of Higher Education* **53** (41). Retrieved 2007-09-04.

o 41. "Quick Takes: Professors Sue Antioch". *Inside Higher Ed*. August 15, 2007. Retrieved 2007-08-15. "

o 42. Antioch College (August 27, 2007). "Antioch Board and University Leadership to Work With Alumni Board". Press release. Retrieved 2007-08-28.

o 43. Antioch College (September 1, 2007). "Antioch College President Steps Down". Press release. Retrieved 2007-09-04.

o 44. Jaschik, Scott (September 4, 2007). "Antioch College President Was Ousted". *Inside Higher Ed*. Retrieved 2007-09-04.
o 45. Jaschik, Scott; Elizabeth Redden (2007-09-06). "Quick Takes: No Confidence Vote at Antioch". Inside Higher Ed. Retrieved 2007-06-09.
o 46. Carlson, Scott (2007-06-29). ""A House Divided"". Retrieved 2007-11-26.
o 47. Chiddister, Diane (2007-11-22). ""Donors balk at perceived lack of College's independence"". The Yellow Springs News. Retrieved 2007-11-22.
o 48. ""Antioch University Trustees Reconfirm Antioch College Suspension"". 2008-02-22. Retrieved 2008-02-22.
o 49. Gottschlich, Stephanie Irwin (2008-03-28). ""Antioch College takeover negotiations fail: University said it needed $12.2 million in cash up front"". Dayton Daily News. Retrieved 2008-03-28.
o 50. Chiddister, Diane (2008-05-11). ""University trustees reject AC3 offer"". The Yellow Springs News. Retrieved 2008-05-11.
o 51. Hannah, James (2008-07-11). "Antioch faculty to keep teaching as school closes". Associated Press. Retrieved 2008-07-16.
o 52. "Liberal Arts Colleges - Tier 3". *America's Best Colleges, 2007*. U.S. News & World Report. Retrieved 2007-06-17. "subscription required"
o 53. Pope, Loren. "Antioch College". Colleges That Change Lives. Retrieved 2007-06-15.
o 54. Will, George (2007-07-15). "Farewell, Antioch". Retrieved 2007-07-17.
o 55. Scott King, Coretta (2004-06-25). "Address". Retrieved 2007-06-15. [3]

Websites (URLs online)

Websites affiliated with Antioch:

o AntiochCollege.org, the current website for Antioch College
o www.antioch-college.edu, Older .edu site will soon redirect to the above .org address until re-accredited.
o Antioch College Alumni Association, the official Antioch College alumni organization.
o Antiochiana, the department of archives and special collections at Antioch College
o The Antioch Record, the College's Newspaper

Unaffiliated websites:

o Antioch University, is no longer directly affiliated with Antioch College but has shared history
o Nonstop Liberal Arts Institute–a project of former Antioch College Faculty, Staff, Students and Alumni
o Yellow Springs News
o The Antioch Papers
o Antioch College Faculty Legal Fund
o The Blaze–An alternative campus publication
o Antioch College Action Network (ACAN)–An independent collective of students, faculty, staff, alumni, villagers and friends of the college
o Listen Up Antioch, a collection of audio and video recordings related to Antioch.
o [4] –Alumni group to pay $6M for Ohio's Antioch College

A hyperlinked version of this chapter is at http://booksllc.net?q=Antioch%5FCollege

4

BRISBANE INDEPENDENT SCHOOL

Educating for Life

- o Established: 1967
- o School type: Independent School
- o Principal: Vicki Bishop
- o Location: Brisbane, Queensland, Australia
- o Campus: Pullenvale
- o Enrolment: 30
- o Homepage: www.bis.org.au
- o

Brisbane Independent School (BIS) is located in semi-rural Pullenvale in the western suburbs of Brisbane, Queensland, Australia.

The community-run school operates within a cooperative family environment. The school is operated and owned by its members, who are the parent body of current students. The school has no religious or other affiliations and thus is one of the few truly independent schools.

Brisbane Independent School's mission is to nurture, develop and trust pupils innate love of learning and positive values, and to produce graduates who are respectful, confident, competent and self-motivated, with the skills necessary for life-long learning in all facets of their lives.

See also (online edition)

- o Democratic school
- o Democracy and Education by John Dewey
- o Alternative education
- o List of schools in Queensland
- o Summerhill School
- o Sudbury model school
- o List of Sudbury schools
- o Non-profit organization
- o Community organisation

Websites (URLs online)

- o Brisbane Independent School Home Page
- o Map
- o Independent Schools Queensland
- o Pine Community School

Coordinates: 27°31 25 S 152°55 09 E / 27.5237°S 152.9191°E / -27.5237; 152.9191

A hyperlinked version of this chapter is at http://booksllc.net?q=Brisbane% 5FIndependent%5FSchool

5

DEMOCRATIC SCHOOL OF HADERA

The **Democratic School of Hadera** is a democratic school in Hadera, Israel. It was founded in 1987 by Yaacov Hecht. With around 380 students aged four to eighteen, it is the largest of the twenty-five Israeli democratic schools.

The school is governed by a weekly school parliament in which all students, teachers, parents and alumni have an equal vote. However, few parents and alumni participate in parliament meetings.

Students are free to decide if they want to attend classes or spend their time on other activities such as music, sports, art, computers, reading, talking, socializing, or doing nothing at all.

In 1993 the first International Democratic Education Conference (IDEC) was held at the Democratic School of Hadera. In 1996 it was held again at that school.

Websites (URLs online)

○ Official Website

Coordinates: 32°25 17.35 N 34°55 21.58 E / 32.4214861°N 34.9226611°E / 32.4214861; 34.9226611

A hyperlinked version of this chapter is at http://booksllc.net?q=Democratic% 5FSchool%5Fof%5FHadera

6

DEMOCRATIC EDUCATION

Part of the Politics series on

- ○ Liberalism
- ○ Development
  Contributions to liberal theory History of Liberalism
- ○ Ideas
  Political liberalism Economic liberalism Cultural liberalism Political freedom Democratic capitalism Democratic education Free trade Individualism Laissez faire Liberal democracy Liberal neutrality Negative / positive liberty Market economy Open society Popular sovereignty Rights (individual) Separation of church and state
- ○ Schools
  American liberalism · Anarcho-liberalism Classical liberalism · Conservative liberalism Democratic liberalism · Green liberalism Libertarianism · Market liberalism National liberalism · Neoliberalism Ordoliberalism · Paleoliberalism Radicalism · Social liberalism
- ○ People
  John Locke Adam Smith Adam Ferguson Thomas Jefferson Thomas Paine David Hume Baron de Montesquieu Immanuel Kant Jeremy Bentham Thomas Malthus Wilhelm von Humboldt John Stuart Mill Thomas Hill Green Leonard Trelawny Hobhouse John

Maynard Keynes Bertrand Russell Ludwig von Mises Friedrich von Hayek · Isaiah Berlin John Rawls · Robert Nozick
o Regional variants
Liberalism worldwide Liberalism in Europe Liberalism in the United States Liberalism by country
o Religious Liberalism
Islamic Liberalism Christian Liberalism Jewish Liberalism
o Organisations
Liberal parties Liberal International International Federation of Liberal Youth (IFLRY)
European Liberal Democrat and Reform Party (ELDR)
Alliance of Liberals and Democrats for Europe (ALDE)
European Liberal Youth (LYMEC)
Council of Asian Liberals and Democrats (CALD)
Africa Liberal Network (ALN) Liberal Network for Latin America (Relial)
o Liberalism portal
o

Democratic education is a theory of learning and school governance in which students and staff participate freely and equally in a school democracy. In a democratic school, there is typically shared decision-making among students and staff on matters concerning living, working, and learning together.

History

The first major writer to discuss a nascent theory of democratic education was Leo Tolstoy who operated his own democratic school for peasant children in Yasnaya Polyana, Russia in the late 19th century.

The primary theorist, however, of what developed into democratic education is John Dewey. His works on the relationship between democracy and education became foundational literature for the broader progressive education movement.

The oldest existing democratic school is the Summerhill School in Suffolk, England founded in 1921. A.S. Neill, its founder, wrote a number of books that now define much of contemporary democratic education theory. Following a critical government inspection in 1999 the then Secretary of State for Education and Employment, David Blunkett issued the school with a 'notice of complaint' over its policy of non-compulsory lessons, a procedure which would usually have led to closure; Summerhill chose to contest the notice[1] which went before a special educational tribunal in the Royal Courts of Justice in London with the school being represented by a noted human rights lawyer, Geoffrey Robertson QC. The government's case soon collapsed and a settlement was offered. This offer was discussed and agreed at a formal school meeting which had been hastily convened in the courtroom from a quorum of pupils and teachers who were present in court. The settlement was much broader than could have been decided on the judge's authority alone as it made provision for Summerhill to be inspected using unique criteria in future which would take account of its special educational philosophy.[2]

Sudbury Valley School, a democratic school founded in Framingham, Massachusetts, United States in 1968, continues to be the model practiced by dozens of Sudbury schools around the world. Certain facets of the Sudbury model separate it from other schools that refer to themselves as "democratic schools" or "free schools." The following features apply to the Sudbury Valley School, see: de-emphasis of classes, age mixing, autonomous democracy, order and discipline, values education, evaluation, the role of adults, diplomas, pluralism and political neutrality, the existence of rules of order, the rule of law, universal suffrage, protecting the rights of individuals.[3][4]

The Albany Free School was established in Albany, NY in 1969 and still operates today. The Albany Free School's founder, Mary Leue, corresponded with Summerhill founder A.S. Neill about her plan to take his experiment of radical freedoms to a different demographic: the inner city. Leue went on to create The Free School in Albany's urban south end with the idea of making these freedoms and democratic principles accessible to children of the poor.

The SchuelerInnenschule, a democratic middle school serving children between the ages of 9 and 19, in Vienna, Austria was founded in 1979 by a small group of parents wanting something different for their children and wanting to follow in the footsteps of the Glockseeschule in Hannover, Germany. At about the same time two ground schools, the Free School of Hofmuehlgasse and the Schulkollektive in WUK, were founded also using the same basic education models. All three of these school are the oldest democratic schools still in existence in Austria.

Since 1993 there has been an International Democratic Education Conference (IDEC) which is held in a different country each year. In 2008, the first EUDEC (European Democratic Education Conference) was held in Leipzig, Germany.

Practice

Pedagogy

Democratic schools do not have compulsory uniform curricula. Instead, these schools place emphasis on learning as a natural product of all human activity. They assume that the free market of ideas, free conversation, and the interplay of people provide sufficient exposure to any area that may prove relevant and interesting to individual students. Students of all ages learn together; older students learn from younger students as well as vice versa. Students of different ages often mentor each other in social skills.

In democratic schools, students are given responsibility for their own education. There is no pressure, implicitly nor explicitly, on students by staff to learn anything in particular. Students are given the right and responsibility to choose what to do with their time and attention.

Because the curricula are different for each student, democratic schools do not compare or rank students. There are no compulsory tests aside from those that individual governments require and those that colleges require for admission.

Some schools mostly in the United States offer a graduation procedure for those who wish to receive a high school diploma. Students who choose to use this option often must present a thesis on how they have prepared themselves for adulthood.

A striking feature of democratic schools is the ubiquity of play. Students of all ages but especially the younger ones often spend most of their time either in free play, or playing games (electronic or otherwise). No attempt is made to limit, control or direct the play it is seen as activity every bit as worthy as academic pursuits, often even more valuable. Play is considered essential for learning, particularly in fostering creativity[5]. The pervasiveness of play has led to a recurring observation by first-time visitors to a democratic school that the students appear to be in perpetual "recess"[6].

Governance

The primary system of governance in a democratic school is a form of direct democracy similar to the New England town meeting. Often, all aspects of governing a democratic school are determined in school meetings. School meetings pass, amend, and repeal school rules, manage the school's budget, and decide on hiring and firing of staff. Each individual present whether student or staff has one vote and most decisions are made by simple majority.

Oftentimes, various aspects of school administration are delegated to parties selected during school meetings. These may include elected administrative clerks (who may be elected from staff or students) and committees of volunteers.

School rules are normally compiled in a law book, updated repeatedly over time, which forms the school's code of law. If a school member commits an infraction, for example by harassing or hurting another member, or by mismanaging a delegated responsibility, the problem is dealt with through the school's judicial system organized by school members. Usually, there is a set procedure to handle complaints, and most of the schools follow guidelines that respect the idea of due process of law. There are usually rules requiring an investigation, a hearing, a trial, a sentence, and allowing for an appeal.

Theory

There is no unified body of literature that spans multiple disciplines in academia on the subject of democratic education. However, there are a variety of spheres of theory that address various elements of democratic education. The goals of democratic education vary according to the participants, the location, and access to resources. Because of this, there is no one widely agreed upon definition.[7]

Political

As a curricular, administrative and social operation within schools, democratic education is essentially concerned with equipping people to make "real choices about fundamental aspects of their lives"[8] and happens *within* and *for* democracy.[9] It "is a process where teachers and students work collaboratively to reconstruct curriculum to include everyone."[10] In at least one conception, democratic education teaches students "to participate in consciously reproducing their society, and conscious social reproduction."[11] This role necessitates democratic education happening in a variety of settings and being taught by a variety of people, including "parents, teachers, public officials, and ordinary citizens." Because of this "democratic education begins not only with children who are to be taught but also with citizens who are to be their teachers."[12] Another definition is noted for its controversy because it views democractic education as "an education that democratizes learning itself."[13]

There are a variety of components involved in democratic education. One author identifies those elements as being a problem-solving curriculum, inclusivity and rights, equal participation in decision-making, and equal encouragement for success.[10] The Institute for Democratic Education identifies the principles of democratic education as,

- o The interaction between democratic philosophy and education,
- o Pluralistic education,
- o School administration by means of democratic procedures,
- o Education based on respect for human rights,
- o Dialogic evaluation,
- o Dialogic relationships, and
- o Critical social thinking.[14]

Sudbury schools contend that values, social justice and democracy included, must be learned through experience[15][16][17][18] as Aristotle said: *"For the things we have to learn before we can do them, we learn by doing them."*[19] They adduce that for this purpose schools must encourage ethical behavior and personal responsibility. In order to achieve these goals schools must allow students the three great freedoms freedom of choice, freedom of action and freedom to bear the results of action that constitute personal responsibility.[20]

The "strongest, political rationale" for democratic education is that it teaches "the virtues of democratic deliberation for the sake of future citizenship."[21] This type of education is often alluded to in the deliberative democracy literature as fulfilling the necessary and fundamental social and institutional changes necessary to develop a democracy that involves intensive participation in group decision making, negotiation, and social life of consequence.

The type of political socialization that takes place in democratic schools is strongly related to deliberative democracy theory. Claus Offe and Ulrich Preuss, two theorists of the political culture of deliberative democracies argue that in its cultural production deliberative democracy requires "an open-ended and continuous learning process in which the roles of both teacher and curriculum are missing. In other words, what is to be learned is a matter that we must settle in the process of learning itself."[22]

The political culture of a deliberative democracy and its institutions, they argue, would facilitate more "dialogical forms of making one s voice heard" which would "be achieved within a framework of liberty, within which paternalism is replaced by autonomously adopted self-paternalism, and technocratic elitism by the competent and self-conscious judgment of citizens."[23]

Edward Portis offers a critique of what he terms democratic education but his use of this term can be better understood as civic education. Portis contends, as many democratic education practitioners and theorists would, that a compulsory curriculum that claims to imbue in its students democratic virtues actually does exactly the opposite. Portis argues that because politics and popular rule is rooted in the public deliberation of competing ideas and conceptions of social life, to pretend that certain values can be taught in the traditional sense through mass compulsory education subverts the democratic nature of the process. There is no such thing as a proper education for democracy in this sense.[24]

Democratic education theorists of the sort whose work underpin democratic schools, rather than those who analyze something akin to civic education (see Gutmann, et al.) would fundamentally agree that democratic values cannot be taught in the traditional sense. If children are to ever learn how to be citizens of a democracy, they must participate in a democracy (see Greenberg 1992).[17] This argument conforms to the cognition-in-context research by Lave below.

In addition, this argument converges with various literatures concerning student voice, youth participation and other elements of youth empowerment.[25][26]

Cultural

One of the first theorists and practitioners of democratic education was the novelist Leo Tolstoy who founded a school for peasant children in Russia.

The most prominent theorist to voice what has become a common justification for uniform, mass-education and critiqued Tolstoy s philosophy, was Émile Durkheim in his lectures at the Sorbonne in 1902-03. Durkheim was the father of modern sociology and developed the sociological/anthropological school of Functionalism. These lectures have since been published under the title *Moral Education*.

Durkheim argued that the transition from primitive to modern societies occurred in part as elders made a conscious decision to transmit what were deemed the most essential elements of their culture to the following generations. In *Moral Education*, Durkheim makes the case for an education system that preserves social solidarity by instilling three principles of secular morality in children: what he terms a spirit of discipline, attachment to social groups, and self-determination. In the process of arguing how to instill these principles, he makes an extended argument on how punishment should be used in the schools. In this section, Durkheim described Tolstoy s theory as an example of a philosophy of education that doesn t seem to use punishment as a mechanism of cultural solidarity formation and transmission:

According to Tolstoy, the model of ideal education is that which occurs when people go on their own initiative to discover things in museums, libraries, laboratories, meetings, public lectures, or simply talk with wise men. In all these cases, there is no constraint exercised; yet do we not learn in this way? Why can t the child enjoy the same liberty? It is then only a matter of putting at his disposal that knowledge deemed useful to him; but we must simply offer it to him without forcing him to absorb it. If such knowledge is truly useful to him, he will feel its necessity and come to seek it himself. This is why punishment is unknown at the school of Iasnaia Poliana. Children come when they wish, learn what they wish, work as they wish.[27]

He then argues that, in fact, punishment is found even in this type of system through subtle mechanisms of social behavior. It should not surprise any students of Durkheim to see how he argues for a social/cultural rather than an individual/rational explanation for punishment and self-regulation:

If the child misbehaves by destroying his playthings the misbehavior is not that he has thoughtlessly and rather stupidly denied himself a way of entertaining himself; rather, it consists in his being insensitive to the general rule that prohibits useless destruction Only disapproval can warn him that not only was the conduct nonsensical but that it was bad conduct violating a rule that should be obeyed. The true sanction, like the true natural consequence, is blame.[28]

Durkheim touches on a point later made by democratic education writer George Dennison in *The Lives of Children*: much social regulation that exists in free society takes place in the course of maintaining our relationships with each other. Our desire to cultivate friendships, engender respect, and maintain what Dennison terms natural authority encourages us to act in socially acceptable ways (i.e. culturally informed practices of fairness, honesty, congeniality, etc.):

The children will feel closer to the adults, more secure, more assured of concern and individual care. Too, their self-interest will lead them into positive relations with the natural authority of adults, and this is much to be desired, for natural authority is a far cry from authority that is merely arbitrary. Its attributes are obvious: adults are larger, are experienced, possess more words, have entered into prior agreements among themselves. When all this takes on a positive instead of a merely negative character, the children see the adults as protectors and as sources of certitude, approval, novelty, skills. In the fact that adults have entered into prior agreements, children intuit a seriousness and a web of relations in the life that surrounds them. If it is a bit mysterious, it is also impressive and somewhat attractive; they see it quite correctly as the way of the world, and they are not indifferent to its benefits and demands.[29]

Durkheim, however, uses this point in the service of an argument for social facts to be communicated through the authority of teachers in traditional formal schools rather than through the natural social relations of democratic life. In fact, he continues his argument on the role of punishment, even the history of corporeal punishment, by demonstrating that it is the product of modern mass-education systems.

Punishment has not always been utilized to teach the right ways of being a member of society. In fact Durkheim cites a number of ethnographies of various hunter-gatherer groups in demonstrating that primitive societies in fact effectively socialized their children without the use of punishment in formal education systems. This evidence has since been confirmed and expanded.[30][31]

Durkheim s ultimate point is that modern societies are so complex so much more complex than primitive hunter-gatherer societies and the roles individuals must fill in society are so varied that formal mass-education is necessary to instill social solidarity and what he terms secular morality .

True education begins only when the moral and intellectual culture acquired by man has become complex and plays too important a part in the whole of the common life to leave its transmission from one generation to the next to the hazards of circumstance. Hence, the elders feel the need to intervene, to bring about themselves the transmission of culture by epitomizing their experiences and deliberately passing on ideas, sentiments, and knowledge from their minds to those of the young.

The dawn of civilization coincided with the dawn of a self-conscious reproduction of social values deemed necessary or essential for social solidarity:

In a word, civilization has necessarily somewhat darkened the child s life, rather than drawing him spontaneously to instruction as Tolstoy claimed. If, further, one reflects that at this point in history violence was common, that it did not seem to affront anyone s conscience, and that it alone had the necessary efficacy for influencing rougher natures, then one can easily explain how the beginnings of culture were signaled by the appearance of corporeal punishment.

Michel Foucault took up the issue of corporeal punishment in his famous works on total institutions. In *Discipline & Punish*, focusing primarily on prisons but including modern schools, Foucault described the transformation of violence since the Enlightenment from a public spectacle to something much more subtle and insidious. Foucault argues that modern schools are used to transmit ideas to the young by claiming a privileged position to declare what is true, normal, and healthy. Rather than resorting to the violence that Durkheim detailed since the dawn of modern mass-education, Foucault argues that corporeal punishment has simply been replaced by forces much more difficult to notice than the force of blows and the whip of belts.[32]

Democratic schools attempt to avoid any form of overt or covert enculturation outside the democratic process. Recognizing that one's 'natural authority' in the eyes of children is ultimately dependent on one's authenticity, teachers at democratic schools avoid tricks and enticements to induce any learning that isn't requested or desired. The only socialization that takes place explicitly is that recognized by the process of democratic deliberation. The fact that a group of individuals students and staff must live, learn, and work together in the same space requires a system of governance. That system, as is the case in most countries and communities that respect principles of human equality, freedom, and the pursuit of happiness, is a form of direct democracy.

Cognitive

The 'practice theory' movement came at a time when there was also a renewed interest in child development and a refining of the theories of Jean Piaget, the foundational child psychologist. Jean Lave was one of the first and most prominent social anthropologists to discuss cognition within the context of cultural settings presenting a firm argument against the functionalist psychology that many educationalists refer to implicitly.

For Lave, learning is a process ungone by an actor within a specific context. The skills or knowledge learned in one process are not generalizable nor reliably transferred to other areas of human action. Her primary focus was on mathematics in context and mathematics education.

The broader implications reached by Lave and others who specialize in situated-learning are that beyond the argument that certain knowledge is necessary to be a member of society (a Durkheimian argument), knowledge learned in the context of a school is not reliably transferable to other contexts of practice.

Economic

Beyond the explicitly political implications, economic implications of democratic education converge with the emerging consensus on 21st century business and man-agement priorities including increased collaboration, decentralized organization, and radical creativity.[33]

Scholars

- o Amy Gutmann - Political scientist, democratic education scholar, President of the University of Pennsylvania
- o A.S. Neill - Democratic education pioneer, founder of the Summerhill School
- o Claus Offe - Political Scientist, theorist of deliberative democratic culture, Hertie School of Governance
- o Émile Durkheim - Sociologist, functionalist education theorist
- o George Dennison - American writer, author
- o Daniel A. Greenberg - One of the founders of the Sudbury Valley School.
- o John Dewey - Social scientist, progressive education theorist, University of Chicago
- o Peter Gray - Psychologist, democratic educaton scholar, Boston College
- o Pierre Bourdieu - Anthropologist, social theorist, College de France
- o Michael Apple - Social scientist, democratic education scholar, University of Wisconsin Madison
- o Michel Foucault - Post-modern philosopher, University of California, Berkeley

See also (online edition)

- o List of democratic schools
- o List of Sudbury schools
- o Constructivism (learning theory)
- o Center for Dewey Studies
- o International Democratic Education Conference* John Dewey Society
- o Rouge Forum

References (URLs online)

- o 1. "Summerhill on trial". *BBC News*. 20 March 2000. Retrieved 2008-01-28.
- o 2. "Summerhill closure threat lifted". *BBC News* (BBC). 23 March 2000.
- o 3. Read description of these features in: Educational philosophy, and Subtleties of a democratic school, Sudbury Valley School.
- o 4. Sadofsky, M. (2009) "What it Takes to Create a Democratic School (What Does That Mean Anyway?)". Lecture, International Democratic Education Conference (IDEC 2008), Vancouver, Canada, "Sustainable Democracy: Creating a Stable Culture in a Democratic School." Retrieved February 3, 2010.
- o 5. http://sudval.org/05_underlyingideas.html#02
- o 6. http://sudval.org/05_underlyingideas.html#08
- o 7. Williams-Boyd, P. (2003) *Middle Grades Education: A Reference Handbook.* ABC-CLIO. p 296.
- o 8. Blacker, D.J. (2007) *Democratic Education Stretched Thin: How Complexity Challenges a Liberal Ideal.* SUNY Press. p 126.
- o 9. Bridges, D. (1997) *Education, Autonomy and Democratic Citizenship: Philosophy in a Changing World.* Routledge. p 76.
- o 10. English, L.D. (2002) *Handbook of International Research in Mathematics Education.* Lawrence Erlbaum Associates. p 21.
- o 11. Gutmann, A. (1987) *Democratic Education.* Princeton University Press. p 321.
- o 12. Gutmann, A. (1987) p 99.

o 13. Gould, E. (2003) *The University in a Corporate Culture.* Yale University Press. p 224.
o 14. "Course for consultants on democratic processes", Institute for Democratic Education. Retrieved 1/13/09.
o 15. Greenberg, D. (1992), Education in America - A View from Sudbury Valley, "'Ethics' is a Course Taught By Life Experience." Retrieved December 22, 2009.
o 16. Greenberg, D. (1987), The Sudbury Valley School Experience, "Teaching Justice Through Experience." Retrieved December 22, 2009.
o 17. Greenberg, D. (1992), Education in America - A View from Sudbury Valley, "Democracy Must be Experienced to be Learned." Retrieved December 22, 2009.
o 18. Greenberg, D. (1987) Chapter 35, "With Liberty and Justice for All," Free at Last The Sudbury Valley School. Retrieved December 22, 2009.
o 19. Bynum, W.F. and Porter, R. (eds) (2005) *Oxford Dictionary of Scientific Quotations.* Oxford University Press. 21:9.
o 20. Greenberg, D. (1987) The Sudbury Valley School Experience "Back to Basics - Moral basics." Retrieved December 22, 2009. 10/27/08.
o 21. Curren, R. (2007) *Philosophy of Education: An Anthology.* Blackwell Publishing. p 163.
o 22. Offe, Claus and Ulrich Preuss. "Democratic Institutions and Moral Resources" "Political Theory Today." David Held, ed. Cambridge: Polity, 1991, 168.
o 23. Offe, Claus and Ulrich Preuss. "Democratic Institutions and Moral Resources" "Political Theory Today." David Held, ed. Cambridge: Polity, 1991, 170-1.
o 24. Portis, E. (2003) "Democratic Education and Political Participation," Paper presented at the annual meeting of the American Political Science Association, Philadelphia Marriott Hotel, Philadelphia, PA. Retrieved 1/15/09.
o 25. Mendel-Reyes, M. (1998) "A Pedagogy for Citizenship: Service Learning and Democratic Education," *New Directions for Teaching and Learning. 73,* pp 31 - 38.
o 26. Sehr, D.T. (1997) *Education for Public Democracy.* SUNY Press. p 178.
o 27. Durkheim, E. (2002). *Moral Education.* New York: Dover, p.178.
o 28. Durkheim, E. (2002). *Moral Education.* New York: Dover, p.179-180.
o 29. Dennison, G. (1999). *The Lives of Children: The Story of the First Street School.* Portsmouth, NH: Boynton/Cook Publishers, 24-5.
o 30. Gray, P., & Ogas, J. (1999). *Summary of results of a survey on hunter-gatherer children s play.* Unpublished manuscript, Boston College.
o 31. Gray, P. Nature s powerful tutors: The educative functions of free play and exploration. *Eye on Psi Chi,* 12 (#1), 18-21. 2007. <http://www.psichi.org/Pubs/Articles/Article_645.aspx⟩
o 32. Foucault, M. (1991). *Discipline and Punish: The Birth of the Prison.* New York: Random House
o 33. Harvard Business Review, (http://blogs.harvardbusiness.org/hamel/2009/02/25_stretch_goals_for_managemen.html)

Websites (URLs online)

o The Online Directory of Democratic Education
o Democratic Learning: The League of Professional Schools
o Peter Gray @ Psychology Today
o Alternative Education Resource Organization (AERO)
o Comprehensive Global List of Democratic Schools (via AERO)

o *The Sudbury Model of Education* by Jeff Collins
o *The Preeminent Intelligence - Social IQ* by Raymond H. Hartjen

Further reading

o Apple, M. (1993) *Official Knowledge: Democratic Education in a Conservative Age.* Routledge.
o Bourdieu, Pierre. (1984) *Distinction: A Social Critique of the Judgment of Taste.* London: Routledge.
o Bourdieu, Pierre and Jean-Claude Passeron. (1990) *Reproduction in Education, Society and Culture.* Theory, Culture and Society Series. Sage.
o Carlson, D. and Apple, M.W. (1998) *Power, Knowledge, Pedagogy: The Meaning of Democratic Education in Unsettling Times.* Westview Press.
o Carr, W. and Hartnett, A. (1996) *Education and the Struggle for Democracy: The politics of educational ideas.* Open University Press.
o Dennison, George. (1999) *The Lives of Children: The Story of the First Street School.* Portsmouth, NH: Boynton/Cook Publishers.
o Dewey, John. (1997) *Experience and Education.* New York: Touchstone.
o Durkheim, Émile. (2002) *Moral Education.* Mineola, NY: Dover.
o Foucault, Michel. (1991) *Discipline and Punish: The Birth of the Prison.* New York: Random House.
o Gatto, John Taylor. (1992) *Dumbing Us Down: The Hidden Curriculum of Compulsory Education.* Philadelphia, PA: New Society.
o Giroux, H. A. (1989) '*Schooling for Democracy: Critical pedagogy in the modern age.* Routledge.
o Gutmann, A. (1999) *Democratic Education.* Princeton University Press.
o Habermas, Jürgen. (1997) "Popular Sovereignty as Procedure "Deliberative Democracy". Bohman, James and William Rehg, eds. Cambridge, MA: MIT Press.
o Held, David. (2006) *Models of Democracy.* Stanford: Stanford University Press.
o Kahn, Robert L. and Daniel Katz. (1978) *The Social Psychology of Organizations.* New York: John Wiley and Sons.
o Kelly, A. V. (1995) *Education and Democracy: Principles and practices.* Paul Chapman Publishers.
o Manin, Bernard. "On Legitimacy and Political Deliberation" Elly Stein and Jane Mansbridge, trans. Political Theory. Vol. 15, No. 3, Aug. 1987: 338-368.
o Neill, A. S. (1995) *Summerhill School: A New View of Childhood.* Ed. Albert Lamb. New York: St. Martin's Griffin.
o Sadofsky, Mimsy and Daniel Greenberg. (1994) *Kingdom of Childhood: Growing up at Sudbury Valley School.* Hanna Greenberg, interviewer. Framingham, MA: Sudbury Valley School Press.

A hyperlinked version of this chapter is at http://booksllc.net?q=Democratic%5Feducation

7

FREE SCHOOL OF EVANSTON

The **Free School of Evanston** was an alternative school that existed in Evanston, Illinois, USA from 1971 to 1976, for five school years.

Influences

The Free School was influenced by Summerhill School. At meetings, parents, students, teachers were all equal, each having one vote. Tuition was based on a sliding scale percentage of parents income. The school did not pursue educational accreditation.

Location

The first year, the school rented space in the in basement of the Evanston Unitarian Church, and for the latter four years in the Wheadon Methodist Church, both on Ridge Ave. in Evanston.

Student body

There were more than 100 students, aged 5 16, divided into lower, middle, and upper age groups, Most were from the Chicago suburbs, but there were also several students from Chicago's inner city neighborhoods.

See also (online edition)

- ○ Free school
- ○ Alternative education
- ○ Student voice

A hyperlinked version of this chapter is at http://booksllc.net?q=Free%5FSchool%5Fof%5FEvanston

8

FREE SCHOOL

Part of the Politics series on

- ○ Anarchism
- ○ Schools of thought
  Agorism · Buddhist · Capitalist Christian · Collectivist · Communist Crypto · Egoist
  Feminist · Free market · Green Heathian · Individualist Infoanarchism · Insurrectionary
  Leftist · Mutualist · Nihilist Pacifist Pananarchist · Philosophical Platformist · Post-
  anarchist Post-colonial · Post-left Primitivist · Social · Socialist · Syndicalist Vegan ·
  Without adjectives · Zen
- ○ Theory · practice
  Anarchy · Black bloc Class struggle · Communes Consensus democracy Decentralization
  · Deep ecology Direct action · Direct democracy Dual power · Especifismo Expropriative
  anarchism · Horizontalidad · Illegalism Individualism · Individual reclamation Isocracy
  · Law Participatory politics Permanent Autonomous Zone Polycentric law Prefigurative
  politics Private defense agency Propaganda of the deed Refusal of work · Rewilding
  Social ecology Social insertion · Spontaneous order
- ○ People
  William Godwin · Josiah Warren · Max Stirner · Johann Most · Pierre-Joseph Proudhon
  · Mikhail Bakunin · Henry David Thoreau · Leo Tolstoy · Peter Kropotkin · Benjamin

Tucker · Errico Malatesta · Emma Goldman · Nestor Makhno · Alexander Berkman · Buenaventura Durruti · Émile Armand · Murray Rothbard · Murray Bookchin · John Zerzan ·
o Issues
Anarcho-capitalism · Animal rights Capitalism · Criticisms · Islam LGBT rights Lifestylism · Marxism · Nationalism Orthodox Judaism · Religion Sex/love Violence
o History
1999 WTO Conference protest 1919 United States anarchist bombings Amakasu Incident Anarchist Catalonia Anarchist Exclusion Act Anarchy in Somalia Australian Anarchist Centenary Barcelona May Days Biennio rosso Carnival Against Capitalism Escuela Moderna · Hague Congress Haymarket affair High Treason Incident Congress of Amsterdam Kate Sharpley Library Kronstadt rebellion Labadie Collection · LIP *Manifesto of the Sixteen* May 1968 · May Day Paris Commune Provo · Red inverted triangle Free Territory of Ukraine
Spanish Revolution Third Russian Revolution Tragic Week · Trial of the thirty
o Culture
Anarchist Bookfair · Anarcho-punk · Arts Black anarchism · Culture jamming DIY culture · Freeganism Independent Media Center Infoshop · *The Internationale* Jewish anarchism · Land and liberty Lifestylism · Popular education Property is theft! Radical cheerleading Radical environmentalism Squatting · Symbolism Terminology · A las barricadas
o Economics
Agorism · Capitalism · Collectivism Communism · Co-operatives Counter-economics · Free market Free school · Free store Geolibertarianism · Gift economy Market abolitionism · Mutual aid Mutualism · Participatory economics Planned Economy Really Really Free Market Self-ownership · Syndicalism Wage slavery Workers' self-management
o By region
Africa · Australia · Austria-Hungary · Brazil Canada · China · Cuba · Ecuador · England France · Greece · India · Iceland · Ireland Israel · Italy · Japan · Korea Mexico · Poland · Russia · Spain Sweden · Turkey · Ukraine United States · Vietnam
o Lists
Anarcho-punk bands · Books Communities · Fictional characters Jewish anarchists · Musicians Organizations · Periodicals · Poets Russian anarchists
o Related topics
Anti-capitalism · Anti-consumerism · Anti-corporatism Anti-fascism · Anti-globalization · Antimilitarism Anti-statism · Anti-war · Autarchism Autonomism · Labour movement Left communism · Libertarianism Libertarian perspectives on revolution
Libertarian socialism Situationist International
o Anarchism Portal Politics portal
o

An anarchistic **free school** (also **anarchist free school** and **free skool**) is a decentralized network in which skills, information, and knowledge are shared without hierarchy or the institutional environment of formal schooling. This organisational structure is distinct from ones used by democratic free schools which permit children's individual initiatives and learning endeavors within the context of a school democracy and from Free education where 'traditional' schooling is made available to pupils without charge.

Overview

Anarchist free schools (or free skool), can be a decentralized network in which skills, information, and knowledge are shared without hierarchy or the institutional environment of formal schooling.

The open structure of this type of free school is intended to encourage self-reliance, critical consciousness, and personal development. These free schools have their roots in the anarchist Escuela Moderna of Spain in the late 19th and early 20th centuries. They are, at heart, non-institutional, non-authoritarian, and counter-cultural. Generally, these are formed at a grassroots level by a group of individuals acting collectively and autonomously to create educational opportunities and promote skill-sharing within their communities. These free schools often operate outside the market economy in favor of a gift economy. Nevertheless, the meaning of the "free" of free schools is not restricted to monetary cost, and can refer to an emphasis on free speech and student-centered education.

History and Philosophy of Anarchist Free schools

Spanish anarchist Francisco Ferrer (1859 1909) established "modern" or progressive schools in Spain in defiance of an educational system controlled by the church. Fiercely anti-clerical, he believed in "freedom in education," education free from the authority of church and state [1]. Murray Bookchin wrote: "This period [1890s] was the heyday of libertarian schools and pedagogical projects in all areas of the country where Anarchists exercised some degree of influence. Perhaps the best-known effort in this field was Francisco Ferrer's Modern School (Escuela Moderna), a project which exercised a considerable influence on Catalan education and on experimental techniques of teaching generally." [2]

Radical experiments in non-hierarchical education with anarchist roots have given rise to temporal and permanent free schools. They are often termed "free skools" to distinguish them from what supporters view as an oppressive and institutional educational industry. Temporal free skools offering skill-shares and training have become a regular part of large radical gatherings and actions. More permanent skools in cities large and small have popped up across North America offering a wide range of workshops, classes, and skill-shares.

Free Skool Santa Cruz in California is perhaps typical of a new batch of free schools that are explicitly rooted in an anarchist tradition of collectivism, autonomy, and self-reliance, and feature informal, non-authoritarian learning outside of the monetary economy. From the Free Skool Santa Cruz website: "More than just an opportunity to learn, we see Free Skool as a direct challenge to dominant institutions and hierarchical relationships. Part of creating a new world is resistance to the old one, to the relentless commodification of everything, including learning and the way we relate to each other."[3]

These are on-going, informal learning networks, that focus on skill-sharing among adults as well as children. The boundaries between students, teachers, and organizers are consciously blurred, with some free skools claiming, "we are all teachers, and we are all students." Free skool "classes" are often autonomous workshops held in informal settings in homes, cafes, and community centers. Free skools typically offer a monthly or quarterly-produced free skool calendar.

Currently active free schools/skools

Australia

- Currambena, NSW
- Melbourne, VIC

Canada

- SEED Alternative School - Toronto, ON

New Zealand

- Tamariki School - Christchurch http://www.tamarikichch.schoolzone.net.nz

United States

- The Village Free School - Portland, OR
- The Seattle FreeSchool - Seattle, WA
- Free Skool Santa Cruz - Santa Cruz, CA
- Experimental College of the Twin Cities - Minneapolis and St. Paul, MN - http://excotc.org
- Mount Pleasant Free School-Mt Pleasant MI
- corvid College- Boston, MA
- Baltimore Free School http://freeschool.redemmas.org/

See also (online edition)

- Alternative education
- Alternative school
- Community High School (Ann Arbor, Michigan)
- DIY ethic
- Direct action
- Democratic education
- Education Otherwise
- Grassroots democracy
- John Taylor Gatto
- Summerhill School A democratic free school established in 1921
- Unschooling

References (URLs online)

- 1. Francisco Ferrer's Modern School
- 2. Chapter 7, *Anarchosyndicalism, The New Ferment*. In Murray Bookchin, *The Spanish anarchists: the heroic years, 1868-1936*. AK Press, 1998, p.115. ISBN 187317604X
- 3. Free Skool Santa Cruz

Websites (URLs online)

- Alternative Education Resource Organization
- Free to Learn - a radical experiment in education (documentary)
- Independent Schools Council Australia
- ABC Radio National program on Progressive Schools in Australia
- RÉPAQ (Réseau des écoles publiques alternatives du Québec)
- The Indypendent: John Tarleton, *Why the Free School Rules*
- The Stelton Modern School - New Jersey, USA
- "The Anarchist Free Space and Free Skool" by Jeff Shantz

A hyperlinked version of this chapter is at http://booksllc.net?q=Free%5Fschool

9

GEORGE DENNISON

George Dennison (1925-1987) was an American novelist and short-story author best known for *The Lives of Children*, his account of the First Street School. He also wrote fiction, plays, and critical essays, most notably his novel *Luisa Domic* and a collection of shorter works, *Pierrot and Other Stories*. Having grown up in a suburb of Pittsburgh, he joined the Navy during World War II, attended the New School for Social Research on the GI Bill, and took graduate courses at New York University.

Although he devoted himself primarily to his art, he also taught school for a number of years, at all levels from preschool to high school. He trained at the New York Institute for Gestalt Therapy with Paul Goodman and later worked with severely disturbed children as a lay therapist and teacher. As an educator he promoted the idea that *relationships, not instruction, promoted real learning.* As such schools needed to be places where freedom of choice created the trust that allows for a full relationship between teachers and students. These ideas were considered radical because they questioned compulsory attendance and the focus on external student behavior to enhance student *management.* Since the focus on controlling student behavior interferes with relationship, his work suggests a preference for small schools and an implied criticism of large schools, especially in their ability to be effective with high risk students. He believe teaching was an art, not really a science and, as such, it was never technique that caused learning to occur, but rather the full complexity of individual relationships between students and teachers that were not reducible to the predictability of technique. Further, he felt that much of significant learning occurs strictly within the students individual motivation and between students, *when the teachers are wise enough to stand aside* and allow it to occur.

His plays were produced at the Hudson Church in New York and elsewhere, and his essays and fiction appeared in many periodicals. In the late Sixties George Dennison and his wife Mabel Chrystie, the founder of the First Street School, moved to rural Maine, where they raised three children.

References (URLs online)

o Obituary at The New York Times
o The Lives of Children (in spanish)

A hyperlinked version of this chapter is at http://booksllc.net?q=George%5FDennison

10

INDIGO SUDBURY CAMPUS

Coordinates: 53°33 22 N 113°34 48 W / 53.55611°N 113.58°W / 53.55611; -113.58

Indigo Sudbury Campus

- Location
- 11004 150th. St. Edmonton, AB Canada
- Information
- Established: 2002
- Grades: K 12 (ungraded, ages 4+)
- Campus: urban
- Philosophy: Sudbury
- Governance: Campus Meeting (democratic, vote by students and staff)
- Website: http://www.indigosudburycampus.com

Main article: Sudbury school

The **Sudbury Valley School** was founded in 1968 in Framingham, Massachusetts, United States. There are now over 35 schools based on the Sudbury Model in the

United States, Canada, Denmark, Israel, Japan, Netherlands, Australia, Belgium and Germany. The model has two basic tenets: educational freedom and democratic governance. The school is attended by children from the ages of 4 to 19.

Educational philosophy

The school's educational philosophy asserts that giving children trust and responsibility at an early age enables them to learn what they want, why they want it, and how to achieve it. Students at the school are free to choose how to spend their time.

Democratic freedom is also a central tenet of the educational philosophy. The school is run by the weekly *Campus Meeting*, which uses a modified form of parliamentary procedure.

School institutions

Campus meeting

Students and staff are invited to participate in the running of the school via the Campus Meeting, with each participant receiving one vote. The meetings are conducted using Robert's Rules of Order. The Campus Meetings determine rules and regulations for all aspects of the school, including finances, new rules, and the election of staff. To keep the school running smoothly, it also creates Clerks, Committees, and Campus Corporations.

Clerks, committees, and corporations

Clerks are essentially administrative officers that handle tasks within the Campus, such as grounds maintenance or attendance records. Committees handle larger tasks, such as school aesthetics or rules violations; the membership of the Judicial Committee is described below, but all other standing committees in the school have open membership – any Campus Meeting Member (staff or student) may join any committee. Campus Corporations are the equivalent of departments or clubs at traditional schools – all Campus Meeting Members (students and staff) may be members of each corporation, and each corporation elects its own directors.[1][2]

The Judicial Committee

The Judicial Committee investigates and deals with allegations of Lawbook violations.

JC basics

- o The JC is made of one staff member and four students.
- o The JC is staffed on a rotating basis.

- Every two weeks the Campus Meeting Chair selects and posts a list of the people who will form the JC.
- The JC meets Mon. - Fri. at 1:00pm unless no JC reports have been written.

JC process

- A student or staff writes a JC report because s/he feels someone has broken a Campus rule.
- At the JC meeting, the person who wrote the report and the person written up can be asked to tell their sides of the story.
- The J.C. votes, after deliberation, if the person written up and/or anyone else involved in the "write up" is to be charged with having broken a Campus law.
- If the person accepts responsibility after being charged by the JC, the accused is invited to determine his/her consequence. If s/he doesn t know what to suggest, the J.C. will deliberate and vote on a suitable consequence.
- A consequence must be passed by a majority vote of the JC.
- If a verdict is appealed, the appeal is held at the weekly Campus Meeting.
- Students and staff alike may be called in front of the Judicial Committee.

Facilities

Following the educational philosophy, the school facilities are somewhat different than most schools. There are no traditional classrooms and no traditional classes, although children are free to request instruction on any subject or talk to any staff member about an interest.[3]

ISC's building was a small neighborhood shopping centre and has been transformed into a series of connected spaces. There are general purpose rooms, as well as specially designated rooms such as a computer room.

Staff

There is no tenure at Indigo Sudbury Campus; an election for staff is held each year. The current staff have been involved professionally with the school for one to eight years.

- Nicolette Groeneveld
- Tim Moore
- Mark Ogle

Curriculum

Curriculum and testing are non-compulsory, so there are no required activities. Students are free to spend their time as they wish, making use of all available resources, including equipment and staff.

Alumni

Sudbury Valley School has published two studies of their alumni over the past thirty-five years. They have learned, among other things, that about 80% of the students continue to study at other schools after graduating from Sudbury Valley. Most alumni have been accepted at the university of their first choice. Students also generally report happiness with their lives, and many have a stated commitment to public service.[4]

Indigo Sudbury Campus has had 8 students graduate from the Campus by going through the thesis procedure, which involves writing and defending a thesis.

References (URLs online)

- o 1. The Sudbury Valley School Handbook
- o 2. The Sudbury Valley School Management Manual
- o 3. Hara Estroff Marano: Psychology Today Magazine: Education: Class Dismissed. May/Jun 2006.
- o 4. Daniel Greenberg, Mimsy Sadofsky, and Jason Lempka The Pursuit of Happiness: The Lives of Sudbury Valley Alumni. Accessed 10 Aug 2006.

See also (online edition)

- o Sudbury model
- o List of Sudbury schools
- o Democratic school
- o Education reform

Additional reading

- o *Free at Last*, by Daniel Greenberg, is a book often read as a first acquaintance with the school and its philosophy.

The Sudbury Valley School Press [1] is an active publishing house managed by the Sudbury Valley School from its campus. Their catalog includes dozens of books, videos and audio recordings about the school.

Websites (URLs online)

- o official website
- o List of Sudbury Schools worldwide

A hyperlinked version of this chapter is at http://booksllc.net?q=Indigo%5FSudbury%5FCampus

11

KILQUHANITY SCHOOL

Coordinates: 55°00 47 N 3°55 41 W / 55.013°N 3.928°W / 55.013; -3.928 **Kilquhanity School** was one of several free schools to have been established in the United Kingdom in the twentieth century. Others include Sands School in Devon, Summerhill in Suffolk and Kirkdale School in London.

The school was founded by John Aitkenhead (1910-1998) [1] [2] and his wife Morag in 1940. It was closed in 1997. It was located near Castle Douglas in Dumfries and Galloway. The school was reopened in 2009 by head teacher and former pupil Andrew Pyle, with the assistance of a Japanese educational organisation Kinokuni Children's Village Schools (headed by Shinichiro Hori). Initially, the school is to have 15 places.

Philosophy

The philosophy of Kilquhanity was heavily influenced by the writing and ideas of A. S. Neill, who founded Summerhill School, where Aitkenhead had worked [1]; essentially that children learn best with freedom from coercion ("free-range").

Further reading

- *The Education Revolution* #32 Spring/Summer 2001 (the magazine of the Alternative Education Resource Organization).
- Various authors. *Summerhill: For and Against*, a collection of essays, arguing both in favour and against Summerhill's (and Kilquhanity's) approach.
- A.S. Neill. *Summerhill*. A book about the school and its philosophy, by the school's founder.

References (URLs online)

- 1. "Obituary: John Aitkenhead". *The Independent*. 1998-08-21. Retrieved 2008-08-22.
- 2. "John Aitkenhead". *Braehead News*. Retrieved 2008-08-22.

Websites (URLs online)

- Official web site
- Alternative school to reopen BBC News channel, March 23, 2009
- Unique school re-opens (*Dumfries and Galloway Standard* article, March 25, 2009)

See also (online edition)

- Free schools
- Democratic school
- Collaborative learning

A hyperlinked version of this chapter is at http://booksllc.net?q=Kilquhanity%5FSchool

12

KIRKDALE SCHOOL

Kirkdale School (1964 - 1980s) was a small, independent free school located in Sydenham, in South London, England at 186 Kirkdale Road. During the whole of the school's existence it was run as a parent/teacher co-operative.

Kirkdale is one of several free schools to have been established in the United Kingdom in the twentieth century. Others include (Sands School in Devon, Summerhill in Suffolk and Kilquhanity School in the Scottish Borders).

Unlike some free schools, Kirkdale was not established in a rural idyll but within a small plot in inner London (Lewisham).

History

The School was founded in 1964 by John and Susie Powlesland and a small group of parents that wanted a radical alternative to the "traditional" UK education system.

Philosophy

The philosophy of Kirkdale was heavily influenced by the writing and ideas of A.S. Neill, who founded Summerhill school; essentially that children learn best with freedom from coercion (free-range). All lessons were optional, and pupils were free to choose what to do with their time. The school had frequent school meetings where pupils and staff alike had an equal voice in the decisions that affected their day-to-day lives, including changing school laws. Meetings were also an opportunity for the community to vote on a course of action, for instance, how to address the actions of one person in relation to another that might be unfair or could even amount to bullying. School meetings were normally weekly, every Wednesday, but extraordinary meetings could be called by anyone (and attendance by all was expected) to address an immediate issue.

Associations

Nick Saunders was involved with Kirkdale. He supported a Summer Camp for the school. A staff member, Romy Fraser, went on to found Neal's Yard Apothecaries with him.

Alumni

o Alistair Hamilton (attended 1973-1976), now has an honours degree in Mechanical Engineering from the University of Bath, and is a European Patent Attorney and amateur horologist, who lives in North Wales - http://www.ahip.co.uk

Further reading

o Powlesland, J. and S. *Kirkdale: an experience in education by self regulation*, Stamboeknummer (2002)
o *The Education Revolution* #32 Spring/Summer 2001 (The Magazine of the Alternative Education Resource Organization).
o Various authors. *Summerhill: For And Against*, A collection of essays, arguing both in favour and against Summerhill's (and Kirkdale's) approach.
o A.S. Neill. *Summerhill*. A book about the school and its philosophy, by the school's founder.

Websites (URLs online)

o http://www.summerhillschool.co.uk

See also (online edition)

o Free schools
o Democratic school
o Collaborative learning

Coordinates: 51°25 44 N 0°03 31 W / 51.4290°N 0.0586°W / 51.4290; -0.0586

A hyperlinked version of this chapter is at http://booksllc.net?q=Kirkdale%5FSchool

13

LIST OF SUDBURY SCHOOLS

Sudbury schools practice a form of democratic education in which students individually decide what to do with their time, and learn as a by-product of ordinary experience rather than through classes or a standard curriculum.[1] Students are given complete responsibility for their own education and the school is run by a direct democracy in which students and staff have an equal vote.

The 'Sudbury' name refers to Sudbury Valley School, founded in 1968 in Framingham, Massachusetts, one of the first schools of this type in North America. The oldest democratic school in existence is the Summerhill School in Suffolk, England, founded in 1921. The Sudbury Valley School has been the inspiration for numerous schools[2] that now informally consider themselves 'Sudbury schools' in addition to being democratic schools.

Australia

- o Booroobin Sudbury Democratic Centre of Learning, City of Caloundra, Queensland

Belgium

o Leerhuis brussel
o Sudbury school Gent

Denmark

o Den Demokratiske Skole, Roskilde

Germany

o Neue Schule Hamburg, Hamburg

Israel

o "Kanaf" Democratic School, Golan Heights
o Sudbury Jerusalem, Jerusalem

Japan

o Kobe Sudbury School, Nishinomiya City
o Democratic School Makkukurosuke, Kanzakigun
o Shonan Sudbury School, Chigasaki-shi
o Okinawa Sudbury School, Ginowan-shi

Netherlands

o De Kampanje, Amersfoort
o De Koers, Beverwijk

United States

o The Diablo Valley School, Concord, California
o Sacramento Valley School, Sacramento, California
o Cedarwood Sudbury School, Santa Clara, California
o Alpine Valley School, Wheat Ridge, Colorado
o River Valley Sudbury School, Chester, Connecticut
o Mountain Laurel Sudbury School, New Britain, Connecticut
o The New School, Newark, Delaware
o Spring Valley School, Palm Harbor, Florida
o Tallgrass Sudbury School, Brookfield, Illinois - established 2008.
o Evergreen Sudbury School, Hallowell, Maine
o Arts & Ideas Sudbury School, Baltimore, Maryland
o Freedom Hill Cooperative, Dickerson, Maryland
o Fairhaven School, Upper Marlboro, Maryland
o Sudbury Valley School, Framingham, Massachusetts
o Clonlara School, Ann Arbor, Michigan

- Longview School, Cortlandt Manor, New York
- Hudson Valley Sudbury School, Kingston, New York
- Katuah Sudbury School, Asheville, North Carolina
- The Circle School, Harrisburg, Pennsylvania
- Clearview Sudbury School, Austin, Texas
- Sego Lily School, Salt Lake City, Utah
- Blue Ridge Sudbury School, Lynchburg, Virginia
- Shenandoah Valley Community School, Harrisonburg, Virginia
- The Trillium School, Indianola, Washington
- The Clearwater School, Bothell, Washington
- Rising Tide School, Olympia, Washington
- Jordan Lake Sudbury School, Cary, NC

Former schools

Belgium

- Sudbury De vlinder (Ghent)

Canada

- Indigo Sudbury Campus, Edmonton, Alberta
- The Beach School (Toronto, Ontario)
- The Fairfield School (Wolfville, Nova Scotia)

United States

- The Chicago Sudbury School (Chicago, Illinois)
- Big Rock SudburySchool (Novato, California)
- Greenwood Sudbury School (Hampton, CT)
- Full Circle Community School (Orlando, Florida)

See also (online edition)

- Sudbury Valley School
- Democratic education
- List of democratic schools

References (URLs online)

- 1. http://www.sudval.org/01_abou_02.html
- 2. "Education:Class Dismissed". Psychology Today. "Since 1991, more than three dozen Sudbury-type schools have sprouted around the country and the world"

A hyperlinked version of this chapter is at http://booksllc.net?q=List%5Fof%5FSudbury%5Fschools

14

LIST OF DEMOCRATIC SCHOOLS

This is a comprehensive list of current and former democratic schools. Most of these were modeled on the Summerhill School, the oldest existing democratic school founded in 1921. This list also includes sub-branches of democratic schools such as Sudbury schools inspired by the Sudbury Valley School and certain free schools that align with the broad principles of democratic education.

Australia

- ○ Alia College (Melbourne)
- ○ Blacktown Youth College (Bidwill)
- ○ Brisbane Independent School (QLD)
- ○ Currambena School (Lane Cove)
- ○ Fitzroy Community School (Melbourne)
- ○ Kinma Primary & Preschool (Sydney)
- ○ Learning Cooperative Hurstbridge (Hurstbridge)
- ○ Pine Community School (Brisbane)
- ○ Preshil, The Margaret Lyttle Memorial School (Melbourne)
- ○ Village School (Melbourne)

Austria

- Die Hupfauer (Monchdorf)
- SchuelerInnenschule im Wuk (Vienna)
- Schulkollektiv Wien Wuk (Vienna)

Belgium

- De Vlinder Sudbury School (Ghent)
- De Weide (Erpe-Mere)
- Leerhuis Brussel (Brussels)

Brazil

- Baniwa School Coripaco Pamáali
- Centro Integrado de Educação de Jovens e Adultos do Campo Limpo (CIEJA) (São Paulo)
- Cidade Escola Aprendiz (São Paulo)
- Escola de Educação Infantil e Ensino Fundamental Teia Multicultural (São Paulo)
- Escola Lumiar (São Paulo)
- Escola Politéia
- Tuyuka School
- Instituto Helena Lubienska/Recanto

Canada

- Agate Private School (London)
- ALPHA Alternative School (Toronto)
- Alternative High School (Calgary)
- Fairfield School (Wolfville)–(closed August 2007[1])
- Indigo Sudbury Campus (South Edmonton)
- The Village Garden School (Kingston)
- Windsor House Alternative Program (North Vancouver)
- Wondertree Learning Center (Vancouver)

Colombia

- Colegio Bilingue Jorge Emilio Gutierrez (Bogota

Costa Rica

- Summerhill Latinoamericano

Denmark

- Det Frie Gymnasium (Kobenhavn)
- Lilleskolernes Sammenslutning

    o Den Demokratiske Skole (Roskilde)

Finland

    o Feeniks-Koulu (Järvenpää)

France

    o Lycee Autogere De Paris (Paris)
    o Lycee Experimental (Saint Nazaire)

Germany

    o Freie Schule Leipzig (Leipzig)
    o Kapriole (Freiburg)
    o Netzwerk-Schule (Berlin)
    o Freie Schule Frankfurt (Frankfurt)
    o Freie Schule Hamburg (Hamburg)

Hungary

    o Carl Rogers Person-Centered School (Budapest)

India

    o Abacus Montessori School (Chennai)
    o Butterflies Program for Street and Working Children (New Delhi)

Indonesia

    o KBKPM (Komunitas Belajar Kampung Pingin Maju) (Kap. Jepara)

Israel

    o Democrati Lev Hasharon (Lev Hasharon)
    o Democratic School of Hadera (Hadera)
    o The Democratic School of Kfar Sava (Kfar-Sava)
    o The Democratic School of Ono Valley (Kiryat-Ono)
    o Dolfin (Eilat)
    o Eynot-Yarden (Upper Galilee)
    o Hashita (Rehovot)
    o Hod Hasharon Democratic School (Hod Hasharon)
    o Jerusalem Sudbury School (Jerusalem)
    o Kanaf Democratic School (Ramat Ha'Golan)
    o Kedem - The Democratic School in Arad (Arad)
    o Kehila - Democratic School in Tel Aviv (Tel Aviv)
    o The Keshet School (Zichron Yaakov)

- Kfar Kera Democratic School (Kfar Kera)
- Korczak Democratic School of Holon (Holon)
- Meitar (Kibbutz Beit Oren)
- Merchav (Ra'anana)
- Nadav - The Modi'in Democratic School (Modi'in)
- The Open Democratic School Jaffa (Tel Aviv)
- Shachaf Democratic School (Shoham)
- Shalem (Upper Galilee)
- Tefen Experimental School (Tefen Industrial State)
- Yafa - The Arab Democratic School (Jaffa)
- Ziv-Kishurit (Kibbutz Kishor)

Japan

- Democraticshool Makkuro-Kurosuke (Kanzakigun)
- Democratic School Sola (Nishinomiya City)
- Global Community School (Takasago City)
- Kinokuni Children's Village (Hashimoto-shi)
- Terakoya Houjousya (Aizuwakamatsu Fukushima)
- Tokyo Shure (Tokyo)
- Shure University(Tokyo)http://shureuniv.org/
- Okinawa Sudbury School (Ginowan City, Okinawa-ken)

Nepal

- Sri Aurobindo Yoga Mandir (Kathmandu)

Netherlands

- Aventurijn School (Loenen)
- De Kampanje (Amersfoort)
- De Koers (Beverwijk)
- De Nieuwe School (Tiel)
- De Paradox (Deventer)
- De Ruimte (Soest)
- De Vallei (Renkum)
- De Vrije Ruimte (Scheveningen)
- Guus Kieft School
- Iederwijs Apeldoorn "Wonderwijs" (Loenen)
- Iederwijs Horst "Hakuna Matata" (Horst)

New Zealand

- Auckland Metropolitan College (Auckland)–(closed December 2001[2])
- Mountain Valley School (Motueka)
- Tamariki School (Christchurch)
- Timatanga (Auckland)

Norway

○ Nyskolen i Oslo

Poland

○ ASSA (Wroclaw)

Portugal

○ Escola da Ponte (Vila Das AVES)

Russia

○ Kluch School (Moscow)
○ Moscow International Film School (Moscow)
○ School for Self-Determination (Moscow)

South Korea

○ Dream School (Seoul)
○ San Children's School (Gyeonggi-Do)
○ School Star (Seoul)
○ Small School (Gwang jin) (Seoul)
○ Small School (Youngsan) (Seoul)
○ Sung Mi San School (Seoul)

Spain

○ Ojo de Agua - Ambiente Educativo

Thailand

○ Moo Baan Dek (Siam)
○ Whispering Seed (Kanchanaburi)

Ukraine

○ Private Secondary Family School AIST (Stork Family School) (Vinnytsia)

United Kingdom

○ the Family School SW London
○ Kirkdale School
○ Malting House School (Cambridge)
○ Park School (Dartington)
○ Rowen House School (Belper)

- ○ Sands School (Ashburton)
- ○ Summerhill School (Leiston)

United States of America

Alabama

- ○ Marietta Johnson School of Organic Education (Fairhope)

Alaska

- ○ School Within a School (East Anchorage High School) (Anchorage)
- ○ Stellar Secondary School (Anchorage)

Arizona

- ○ A Full Table (Sahuarita)
- ○ Highland Free School (Tucson)

California

- ○ Cedarwood Sudbury School (Santa Clara)
- ○ Diablo Valley School (Concord)
- ○ Deep Springs College (Deep Springs)
- ○ Global Village School (Ojai)
- ○ Manzanita School (San Luis Obispo)
- ○ Play Mountain Place (Los Angeles)
- ○ Sacramento Valley School (Sacramento)
- ○ Wildcat Community FreeSchool (Richmond)

Colorado

- ○ Boulder Valley Community Open School (Boulder)
- ○ Alpine Valley School (Wheat Ridge)
- ○ Eagle Rock School (Estes Park)
- ○ Jefferson County Open School (Lakewood)
- ○ The Patchwork School (Louisville)

Connecticut

- ○ Mountain Laurel Sudbury School (New Britain)

Delaware

- ○ The New School (Newark)

Florida

- Grassroots School (Tallahassee)
- SAIL High School (Tallahassee)
- School Without Walls (Live Oak)
- Spring Valley School (Palm Harbor)
- Stonesoup School (Crescent City)

Georgia

- Horizons School (Atlanta)

Hawaii

- Sudbury Maui (Haiku)

Indiana

- Harmony Education Center (Bloomington)

Maine

- The Community School (Camden)
- The Discovery School (Lewiston)
- The New School (Kennebunk)
- River School (Belfast)
- School Around Us (Arundel)

Maryland

- Fairhaven School (Upper Marlboro)
- Freedom Hill Cooperative (Dickerson)
- Arts & Ideas Sudbury School (Baltimore) [1]

Massachusetts

- Balance Rock Center (Jefferson)
- School Within a School (Brookline High School) (Brookline)
- Stone Soup School (Worcester)
- Sudbury Valley School (Framingham)

Michigan

- Clonlara School (Ann Arbor)

Minnesota

- Second Foundation School (Minneapolis)

New Hampshire

o Ashuelot River Free School (Winchester)
o The Community School (South Tamworth)
o The Meeting School (Rindge)
o Woodland Community School (Bethlehem)

New Jersey

o Emerson Lily Free School (Stanhope)
o The Teddy McArdle Free School (Little Falls)
o Voyagers Community School (Colts Neck)
o Wellspring Community School (Gladstone)

New Mexico

o The Tutorial School (Sante Fe)

New York

o Academic Community for Educational Success (Bedford Hills)
o Brooklyn Free School (Brooklyn)
o Albany Free School (Albany)
o First Street School (Manhattan)
o Harriet Tubman Free School (Albany)
o Hudson Valley Sudbury School (Kingston)
o Lehman Alternative Community School (Ithaca)
o Little River Community School (Canton)
o Longview School (Cortlandt Manor)
o Manhattan Free School (Manhattan)
o Scarsdale Alternative School (Scarsdale)
o School Without Walls (Rochester)

North Carolina

o Arthur Morgan School (Burnsville)
o Katuah Sudbury School (Fletcher)
o Raleigh Progressive School and Learning Center (Raleigh)

Ohio

o Antioch College

Oregon

o Trillium Charter School (Portland)
o The Village Free School (Portland)

Pennsylvania

- The Circle School (Harrisburg)
- Upattinas School and Resource Center (Glenmoore)

Puerto Rico

- Casa Sudbury (Cidra)
- Espacio A (San Juan)

Rhode Island

- The Metropolitan Regional Career and Technical Center (Providence)

Tennessee

- The Farm School (Summertown)
- Laurel High School (Knoxville)

Texas

- The Real School AKA Dragon Valley (Houston)

Utah

- Sego Lily School (Salt Lake City)

Vermont

- Red Cedar School (Bristol)

Virginia

- ARCH Academy (Staunton)
- Blue Ridge Sudbury School (Lynchburg)
- H-B Woodlawn Program (Arlington)
- The New School of Northern Virginia (Fairfax)
- Shenandoah Valley Community School (Harrisonburg)

Washington

- The Clearwater School (Bothell)
- Puget Sound Community School (Seattle)
- The Trillium School (Indianola)

West Virginia

○ The Highland School (Highland)

Wisconsin

○ The Young Women's Institute for Global Studies (Milwaukee)

See also (online edition)

○ Democratic education
○ List of Sudbury schools
○ Collaborative learning
○ Constructionist learning
○ Rouge Forum

References (URLs online)

○ 1. http://www.novanewsnow.com/article-134708-Fairfield-School-closes.html
○ 2. http://www.nzcer.org.nz/default.php?products_id=554

A hyperlinked version of this chapter is at http://booksllc.net?q=List%5Fof%5Fdemocratic%5Fschools

15

MALTING HOUSE SCHOOL

The **Malting House School** (also known as the **Malting House Garden School**) was an experimental educational institution that operated from 1924 to 1929. It was set up by the eccentric and, at the time, wealthy Geoffrey Pyke in his family home in Cambridge and it was run by Susan Sutherland Isaacs. Although it was open for only a few years, the radical ideas explored in this institution have remained influential up until the present day.

Creation

Geoffrey and Margaret Pyke had a son, David (1921 2001). Geoffrey Pyke became preoccupied by the question of his son's education. He wanted to create an education that promoted curiosity and equipped young people to live in the twentieth century an education that would be utterly different to his own unhappy experience. To do this he set up an infants' school in his Cambridge home. Founded in October 1924, the school was funded by Pyke's City speculations. His wife, Margaret, was a strong supporter of the school and its ideas.

Pyke placed advertisements in a number of journals, including the New Statesman and Nature:

WANTED an Educated Young Woman with honours degree preferably first class or the equivalent, to conduct education of a small group of children aged 2-1/2 7, as a piece of scientific work and research.

Previous educational experience is not considered a bar, but the advertisers hope to get in touch with a university graduate or someone of equivalent intellectual standing who has hitherto considered themselves too good for teaching and who has probably already engaged in another occupation. <

A LIBERAL SALARY liberal as compared with research work or teaching will be paid to a suitable applicant who will live out, have fixed hours and opportunities for a pleasant independent existence. An assistant will be provided if the work increases.

They wish to obtain the services of someone with certain personal qualifications for the work and a scientific attitude of mind towards it. Hence a training in any of the natural sciences is a distinct advantage.

Preference will be given to those who do not hold any form of religious belief but this is not by itself considered to be a substitute for other qualifications.[1]

Pyke recruited psychologist Susan Sutherland Isaacs to run the school; although Pyke had many original ideas regarding education, he promised her that he would not interfere.

Both Pyke and Isaacs had had unconventional and unhappy experiences of growing up. Pyke's father, Edward Lionel Pyke, was a Jewish lawyer who died when he was only five years old, leaving his family with no money. His mother quarrelled with relatives and made life "hell" for her children. She sent Geoffrey to Wellington, a snobbish private school mainly catering to the children of Army officers; here, she insisted that Pyke maintain the dress and habits of an Othodox Jew. There he was a victim of persecution that instilled him with a hatred of and contempt for the establishment.[2] After two years at Wellington, he was withdrawn, tutored privately and then admitted to Pembroke College, Cambridge to study law.[3] Isaacs mother died when she was six years old. Shortly afterwards she became alienated from her father after he married the nurse who had attended her mother during her illness. At the age of fifteen, Isaacs was removed from school by her father because she had converted to atheistic socialism; her father refused to speak to her for 2 years. She stayed at home with her stepmother until she was 22.[4]

Besides Geoffrey Pyke and his wife, the other leading figures in the school were Susan Isaacs's and her second husband, Nathan Isaacs; and Evelyn Lawrence who arrived two years into the experiment.[5]

In April 1927, the school advertised again:

WANTED A SCIENTIST of the first order, if necessary of senior standing, but as young as possible, with a knowledge of the theory of science, to investigate and conduct the introduction of young children, $4\frac{1}{2}$ 10, to science and scientific method.[6]

This advertisement indicated that Ernest Rutherford, Percy Nunn and J.B.S. Haldane had agreed to assist the directors of the school in the final selection of candidates.

Operation

In an advertisement for residential pupils, in July 1927, some of the operating princilples of the school were explained.

The method employed at Cambridge with children ranging from 3 to 7 to forward this result is on the one hand to eliminate the arbitrary authority of the pedagogue and to substitute for it the attitude of the co-investigator ("Let's find out" and not on any verbal information is the answer given to most questions), and on the other hand to provide an environment with more than usual scope for activity, intellectual and social, including apparatus which shall both set problems and provide their solution. For instance: a lathe, simulative poser of many arithmetical and geometrical questions apparatus showing the expansion of materials under heat where nothing visible may happen except with patience a garden with plants (which may without taboo be dug up every day to see how they are getting on, leading mainly to the discovery that that is a temptation best resisted if growth is desired) animals which breed weighing machines graded from a see-saw with weights, through kitchen scales, to a laboratory balance typewriters to bridge the gap between writing and reading double-handed saws which compel cooperation and clay for modelling, where phantasy pays toll to skill and effort.[6]

It seems very likely that the form of education was influenced by the ideas of John Dewey. In the 1920s and 30s, John Dewey became famous for pointing out that the authoritarian, strict, pre-ordained knowledge approach of traditional education was too concerned with delivering knowledge, and not enough with understanding students' actual experiences. The Malting House School fostered the individual development of children; children were given great freedom and were supported rather than punished. The teachers were seen as observers of the children who were seen as research workers.

...Dan (5;1) was looking at a picture of a steamship, and Mrs. I. made some remark about "the windows". Dan corrected her, emphatically, "They're not windows, they're *portholes*". Mrs. I. said, "Yes, they're portholes, but then portholes *are* windows". (He had not at that date seen any actual steamships, only pictures of them.) Dan rejected this "egocentrically", and with vehement scorn. But when Mrs. I. suggested that he should ask Christopher, who, as Dan knew had come over from America on a steamship, he did so, and meekly accepted Christopher's corroboration of Mrs. I.'s statement.[7]

The children had a bonfire of rubbish in the garden, and they remarked on the volume of smoke coming from it, and called themselves "brave" when they ran through it. Dan (5;2) [five years and two months] said "It makes me choke when it goes down inside". He asked, "Is there any soot in the smoke?" Mrs I[saacs] replied "Let's hold something in it and see". They held a white plate in the smoke; a thin brown film was deposited, and the children said, "Yes, there *is* soot in it". Mrs I. then took a candle, lit it, and held the plate in the smoke from it. The children said, on seeing the much heavier deposit of soot, "There's *much* more soot in that". Dan said, "You've burnt the plate". Mrs I. washed the plate, and he saw that the soot came off and that the plate itself was not burnt.[8]

Closure

At the end of 1927, Susan Isaacs left the school. It is not clear exactly why Susan Isaacs left, one possibility is that Pyke began to interfere with the day-to-day running of the school[4] but the developing emotional and sexual tangle of relationships between Susan Isaacs, Nathan Isaacs and Evelyn Lawrence may also have been a factor. Evelyn would become Nathan's second wife after Susan's death in 1948.[5]

In 1927, Pyke lost all his money.[9] The Maltings School was forced to close, Margaret Pyke had to take a job as headmistress's secretary; she left Geoffrey although they were never divorced. Already suffering from periodic fits of depression and burdened with huge debts to his brokers, he now withdrew from normal life altogether and existed on donations from his close friends.

Influence

For a short time The Maltings was a critical if not a commercial success; it was visited by many educationists and it was the subject of a film documentary.

Visitors to the school included Jean Piaget and Melanie Klein.[10]

References (URLs online)

Notes

- 1. Drummond quotes Pykes advertisement Mary Jane Drummond. "Comparisons in Early Years Education: History, Fact, and Fiction". *Early Childhood Research and Practice*. Retrieved 30 June 2008.
- 2. Perutz, 2002, p85.
- 3. Pyke, 2002, pp16-17.

- 4. Mary Jane Drummond. "Comparisons in Early Years Education: History, Fact, and Fiction". *Early Childhood Research and Practice*. Retrieved 30 June 2008.
- 5. Cameron, 2006, p853-854.
- 6. Wanted A Scientist of the first order... (Advertisement), The Times newspaper, 26 April 1927 p10 column E.
- 7. Isaacs 1930, p91.
- 8. Isaacs 1930, p133.
- 9. Lampe, 1959, pp35-36, 51-53.
- 10. Cameron, 2006, p853

General references (URLs online)

- Isaacs, Susan (1960) [1930]. *Intellectual Growth In Young Children.* Appendix by Nathan Isaacs. London: Routledge & Kegan Paul.
- Lampe, David (1959). *Pyke, the Unknown Genius.* London: Evans Brothers.
- Perutz, Max (2002 - paperback). *I Wish I Made You Angry Earlier.* Oxford University Press. ISBN 0-19-859027-X.
- Pyke, Geoffrey (2002). *To Ruhleben and Back.* Collins Library. McSweeny's Books. ISBN 0-9719047-8-2.
- Cameron, Laura (2006). "Science, nature, and hatred: 'finding out' at the Malting House Garden School, 1924-29" (PDF). *Society and Space* (Environment and Planning) **24**: 851 872. Retrieved 11 June 2008.

Further reading

Websites (URLs online)

A hyperlinked version of this chapter is at http://booksllc.net?q=Malting%5FHouse%5FSchool

16

ROWEN HOUSE SCHOOL

Rowan House School

- **Established**: 1979
- **Closed**: 4 Feb 1992[1]
- **Type**: Democratic education
- **Headteacher**: Bryn Purdy
- **Founders**: Bryn Purdy
- **Location**: 50 Holbrook Road Belper Derbyshire DE56 1PB England
- **LEA**: Derbyshire
- **Gender**: Girls
- Coordinates: 53°00 55 N 1°28 42 W / 53.0154° N 1.4782° W / 53.0154; -1.4782

Rowen House was an independent British boarding school founded in 1979 in Belper, Derbyshire. The name was not a mis-spelling, but a reference to the Utopian thinker and eutopian practitioner, Robert Owen. This "educational experiment" utilised the power of the childhood group like Summerhill School.[2]

Principles

It was based on the principles developed by Alexander Sutherland Neill at Summerhill School, in turn deriving from those pioneered by Homer Lane in his Little Commonwealth. The children which it served were however substantially different. Summerhill children were those of fee-paying parents, who patronised it for ideological reasons. Rowen House was funded by state education authorities looking for respite care for behaviourally disordered girls from usually socially deprived backgrounds. A particularly apt phrase has been coined for them "school phobic". Moreover they were largely entering their teenage years.

Nevertheless the basic Summerhill principles applied. That even children who resist being taught have an appetite to learn. Moreover, will learn self-control in an environment free of imposed control, where it is negotiated within a mutually supportive social community. In other words, democracy instead of authoritarianism.

Background

Its head, Bryn Purdy, had worked at Summerhill and, later, with Wills in his Bromley project. After this, he applied its principles in an inner city "special" school set up by the Local Education Authority for day pupils.

As Shotton[3] was later to write *What unites the Little Commonwealth . . . and Rowen House . . . is the importance attached to personal autonomy, the aversion to systems of reward and punishment, hostility to coercive pedagogy and the fundamental and central belief in [shared responsibility].*

However, in the 'seventies, control of state education became more centralised, with more emphasis on what could be termed behaviourist principles. Accordingly, it became increasingly difficult to maintain the semi-formal approach to engaging the children in learning and self-discipline.

The school

Accordingly, Bryn Purdy and his wife bought a former orphanage in Belper to develop as an independent school to which various local authorities might refer children, specifically adolescent girls, who were finding it impossible to progress in more conventional educational settings.

Such children may have been subjected to a family background of neglect or violence, and to sustained bullying at school, to which they have reacted in the only way they knew how. As Purdy puts it *"a teacher, through his or her headteacher, will bring the child to the attention of an educational psychologist, who may engage the help of a social worker. Then, after five years or so, when the child is at the end **no**, when the child has **cut** his tether the psychiatrist will call a Case Conference the odd headteacher or social worker, or educational psychologist, who cares for the* *individual child, will press for his or her welfare, and, eventually, the child will arrive at our school."*

Purdy uses the term "unschool" *"When a child has suffered failure, for whatever reason, at school or at home, we feel that we must offer her something different, perhaps radically different, from the arena of failure in the past We aim to enter into as egalitarian a relationship with her as possible. One of the means of achieving this is to hold an assembly each day which we call the 'Moot'."*[4]

The "Moot" was the morning meeting central to the school day, where each individual felt free to raise any issues that concerned it. Unlike other previous schools, such as the "Little Commonwealth", fining was not imposed for misdemeanours, since the children had virtually no money. Instead restitution was sought and agreed with the other children.

Initially characterised by outbursts of shouting and emotionality, frequently bordering on violence, as Purdy [5] puts it *Each day, week, month, brought less shouting, less wrangling; more rationality, more humour. The character of the Moot changed from a judicial 'court' to an exercise of conviviality, a daily conversation between friends.*

Although classes were voluntary, most children attended at least some of them most of the time and since each child was there voluntarily the lessons tended to be productive. Among the many parents, teachers, educationalists[2] was an MP who felt moved to express praise in Parliament.[6]

A number went on to attend a local college part time to progress to 'A' level and, after leaving, some have gained degrees at university.

With the Education Reform Act 1988 however, introduction of the National Cur-riculum became compulsory. The Inspectorate of Schools insisted that the Moot be removed from the timetable and that attendance at class be compulsory. This was exactly the environment that the children had come from, and with which they had been unable to cope. While schools like Summerhill were sufficiently well known and well connected to continue (and recently won a ground-breaking tribunal appeal[7]) it became impossible for Rowen House to continue.

References (URLs online)

- 1. School index
- 2. The Nurture Assumption Why Children Turn Out The Way They Do, Judith Rich Harris, 1999, ISBN 0 68485 707 3, accessed June 2009.
- 3. Shotton, .,(1993) *No Master Highor Low* Bristol: Libertarian Education
- 4. Purdy, B., (1989) *Girls Will be Grils: A Fictive Documentary About a Community of Adolescent Girls Under Stress,* Belper: Llaneill Press.
- 5. Purdy. B., (1997) *A.S.Neill: Bringing happiness to some few children,* Nottingham: *Educational Heretics Press.*

○ 6. Hansard.
○ 7. "Summerhill closure threat lifted". *BBC News* (BBC). 2000-03-23.

A hyperlinked version of this chapter is at http://booksllc.net?q=Rowen%5FHouse%5FSchool

17

SANDS SCHOOL

Coordinates: 50°31 00 N 3°45 09 W / 50.5165758295837°N 3.7525713443756°W / 50.5165758295837; -3.7525713443756104

Sands School

- o **Established**: 1987
- o **Type**: Independent democratic Day School
- o **Location**: 48 East Street Ashburton Devon TQ13 7AX England
- o **LEA**: Devon
- o **Ofsted number**: 113619
- o **Staff**: approx 8 teaching, 5 support
- o **Students**: approx 50 - 70 students
- o **Gender**: Coeducational
- o **Ages**: 11 to 18
- o **Website**: www.sands-school.co.uk

Sands School is a democratic school in Ashburton, Devon in England

History

Sands School was started in 1987 by a group of students and teachers from the recently closed Dartington Hall School. Starting in the kitchen of a parent's house, the school quickly established its own philosophy, building on the progressive principles of Dartington. The school's name, Sands, comes from the first letters of the first names of two of the founding teachers, Sean Bellamy and Sybilla Higgs: S and S , or 'Sands'. This shortening came from the letters written by the school's other founding teacher, David Gribble, to Sean and Sybilla in the spring and summer of 1987. The school grew from its original size of 17, and within six months had moved to a large town house in Ashburton where it is still based today. Since 1991 it has been at the forefront of the international democratic education movement worldwide [IDEC] and has partner schools in Israel, Japan, U.S.A and most European countries. In 2006 the European branch of this movement was launched[EUDEC] and many Sands students are actively involved in promoting democratic approaches to education both in the Private and State sector in this country and abroad, travelling through Europe to conferences and events aimed at establishing democratic education as a viable alternative to the present educational model. At the heart of the model is the idea that students should help design their place of learning and remain actively involved in the making of its rules and contributing to its philosophy; that students and teachers should all exist as equal partners in the running of the school and that students should map their own route through their school careers with guidance from the adults. The result is a place where play is still important even to 16 year olds, where talking is valued as is recreation and where students tend to be relaxed, happy and well behaved in class mainly because they have made the conscious decision to attend their classes without coercion. Sands School is run by the School Meeting[comprising all students and staff and has ultimate say in school affairs] and the School Council[6 elected students and an elected teacher who investigate and advise on daily events, feeding information back to the whole school for action and decisions] Since the closure of Dartington Hall School in 1987 and its junior section Aller Park earlier in the 80's only Sands and Summerhill exist as long-lived examples of democratic education in this country. New schools are beginning to surface and even in the present results-obsessed climate the UK is witnessing a renewed interest in Human Scale and Democratic education.

Websites (URLs online)

- o Sands School
- o International Democratic Education Network
- o Phoenix Education Trust

A hyperlinked version of this chapter is at http://booksllc.net?q=Sands%5FSchool

18

SUDBURY VALLEY SCHOOL

The Sudbury Valley School

- Location
- 2 Winch Street Framingham, MA United States
- Information
- Established: 1968
- Faculty: 10
- Grades: K 12 (ungraded, ages 4+)
- Number of students: 160 200
- Campus size: 10 acres
- Campus: suburban
- Philosophy: Sudbury
- Governance: School Meeting (democratic, vote by students and staff)
- Website: http://www.sudval.org

The **Sudbury Valley School** was founded in 1968 in Framingham, Massachusetts[1], United States. There are now over 30 schools based on the Sudbury Model in the United States, Denmark, Israel, Japan, Netherlands, Belgium and Germany[2]. The model has two basic tenets: educational freedom and democratic governance. It is a private school, attended by children from the ages of 4 to 19.

Sudbury Valley School practice a form of democratic education in which students individually decide what to do with their time, and learn as a by-product of ordinary experience rather than through classes or a standard curriculum.[3] Students are given complete responsibility for their own education and the school is run by a direct democracy in which students and staff are equals.

Educational philosophy

Certain facets of the Sudbury model separate it from other schools that refer to themselves as "democratic schools" or "free schools." The following features apply to the Sudbury Valley School:[4]

- o **De-emphasis of classes:** classes arise only when an individual creates them, and staff are not expected to offer classes as any sort of curriculum most democratic schools offer at least some basic curricula. Sudbury schools' attitude on classes stems from the belief that every individual learns what they need to know through life and that there is no need to try and design a curriculum that will prepare a young person for adult life. Thus protecting one of the rights of the students in this school, the right of self determination.[5]
- o **Age mixing:** students are not separated into age-groups of any kind and allowed to mix freely, interacting with those younger and older than themselves; free age-mixing is emphasized as a powerful tool for learning and development in all ages.
- o **Autonomous democracy:** another prominent difference is the limitation or total absence of parental involvement in the administration of Sudbury schools; Sudbury schools are run by a democratic School Meeting where the students and staff participate exclusively and equally. Members of these schools learn democracy by experience, and enjoy the rights of individuals and the three freedoms that constitute personal responsibility freedom of choice, freedom of action, freedom to bear the results of action.[6][7] Remarkably, the democratic School Meeting of a Sudbury school is also the sole authority on hiring and firing of staff. These facets also separate these schools from most others.
- o **Order and discipline:** is achieved by a dual approach based on a free and democratic framework: a combination of popularly-based authority, when rules and regulations are made by the community as a whole, fairly and democratically passed by the entire school community, supervised by a good judicial system for enforcing these laws – due process of law; and developing internal discipline in the members of the community by enhancing their ability to bear responsibility and self-sufficiency.[8]
- o **Values education:** Sudbury schools choose to recognize that students are personally responsible for their acts, in opposition to virtually all schools today that deny it. The denial is threefold: schools do not permit students to choose their course of action fully; they do not permit students to embark on the course, once chosen; and they do not permit students to suffer the consequences of the course, once taken. Freedom of choice, freedom of action, freedom to bear the results of action these are the three great freedoms that constitute personal responsibility. Sudbury schools claim that *"Ethics" is a course taught by life experience.* They adduce that the absolutely essential ingredient for acquiring values and for moral action is personal responsibility, that schools will

become involved in the teaching of morals when they become communities of people who fully respect each others' right to make choices, and that the only way the schools can become meaningful purveyors of ethical values is if they provide students and adults with real-life experiences that are bearers of moral import.[9][10][11]

o **Evaluation:** Sudbury schools do not perform and do not offer evaluations, assessments, or recommendations, asserting that they do not rate people, and that school is not a judge; comparing students to each other, or to some standard that has been set is for them a violation of the student's right to privacy and to self-determination. Students decide for themselves how to measure their progress as self-starting learners as a process of self-evaluation: real life-long learning and the proper educational evaluation for the 21st Century, they adduce.[12] According to Sudbury schools, this policy does not cause harm to their students as they move on to life outside the school. However, they admit it makes the process more difficult, but that such hardship is part of the students learning to make their own way, set their own standards and meet their own goals. The no-grading and no-rating policy helps to create an atmosphere free of competition among students or battles for adult approval, and encourages a positive co-operative environment amongst the student body.[13]

o **The role of adults:** the school is organized to allow freedom from adult interference in the daily lives of students. As long as children do no harm to others, they can do whatever they want with their time in school. The adults in other schools plan a curriculum of study, teach the students the material and then test and grade their learning. The adults at Sudbury schools are *"the guardians of the children's freedom to pursue their own interests and to learn what they wish,"* creating and maintaining a nurturing environment, in which children feel that they are cared for, and that does not rob children of their time to explore and discover their inner selves. They also are there to answer questions and to impart specific skills or knowledge when asked to by students.[14][15][16]

o **Diplomas:** The Sudbury Valley School is fully accredited to award a High School Diploma; though within the community of Sudbury schools and within Sudbury Valley itself, it is a matter of some controversy, given the stance against evaluation. Each student seeking a diploma writes on the topic of how they have prepared themselves for adulthood and entering the community at large. The thesis is reviewed, along with a copy of the students' judicial record and attendance record, by three staff members from other Sudbury schools, who meet with the student seeking a diploma and decide whether or not to the standards for receiving a diploma have been met.[17]

o **Pluralism:** The Sudbury Valley School does not espouse nor endorse any political tenet. They are not tied to any political or economic movements, except for its commitment to let children be autonomous within the school. Unlike virtually all other schools, Sudbury Valley does not encourage involvement by its students in particular causes or social movements, relying on the free market of ideas to lead students towards actions and movements that they respond to.[18]

School institutions

School meeting

Students and staff are invited to participate in the running of the school via the School Meeting, with each participant receiving one vote. The meetings are conducted using Robert's Rules of Order. The School Meetings determine rules and regulations for all aspects of the school, including finances, new rules, and the election of staff. To keep the school running smoothly, it also creates Clerks, Committees, and School Corporations.

Clerks, committees, and corporations

Clerks are essentially administrative officers that handle tasks within the school, such as grounds maintenance or attendance records. Committees handle larger tasks, such as school aesthetics or rules violations; the membership of the Judicial Committee is described below, but all other standing committees in the school have open membership any School Meeting Member (staff or student) may join any committee in the first ten days of October or the first ten days of January. School Corporations are the equivalent of departments or clubs at traditional schools all School Meeting Members (students and staff) may be members of each corporation, and each corporation elects its own directors.[19][20]

The Judicial Committee

The Judicial Committee investigates allegations of school rules violations, holds a trial, determines a verdict, and imposes a sentence (much like the current judicial system in the United States).[21] If a verdict is appealed, the appeal is held in the weekly School Meeting. Students and staff alike may be called in front of the Judicial Committee.

School assembly

There is also an annually-held School Assembly, which is the broad policy-making arm of the school.[22] It consists of staff, students, and parents of students. Its main purpose is to approve the school budget submitted by the School Meeting. It also elects a Board of Trustees, which only exist in an advisory capacity.[23] Its purpose is to study questions posed to it by the Assembly and report back to the Assembly when it is ready to do so.

Facilities

Following the educational philosophy, the school facilities are somewhat different from most schools. There are no traditional classrooms and no traditional classes, although children are free to request instruction on any subject or talk to any staff member about an interest.[24]

The main school building is a large Victorian-style mansion. There are many general purpose rooms, as well as specially designated rooms such as reading rooms, music rooms, etc. There are also several outbuildings, with facilities for woodworking and other activities. The 10-acre (40,000 m^2) grounds house hills, woods, a traditional playground, and a large pond. Computers with internet access and video games are also accessible.

Staff

There is no tenure at Sudbury Valley School they adduce it keeps them all on their toes and being effective with students. The school Meeting, with each participant receiving one vote, hires staff, as part of its duties in running the school. Every year, in the Spring, elections are held for next year's staff. Anyone who wants to serve has to place their names in nomination. The school Meeting debates the school's staff needs at length, and discusses each candidate in turn. On election day, everyone at school, student and staff member, has a chance to vote by secret ballot. In spite of this, they assert the kind of commitment to an institution that Sudbury Valley's staff has is absolutely unique: a commitment to seeing Sudbury Valley flourish. The current staff have been involved professionally with the school for two to forty years.[25]

- o Mach Bell, singer with Mach 5, formerly with Thundertrain [26]
- o Denise Geddes
- o Scott David Gray
- o Daniel Greenberg, a founder
- o Hanna Greenberg, a founder
- o Mikel Matisoo
- o Morningstar Medaye
- o Tay Arrow Parker
- o Joan Rubin, a founder
- o Mimsy Sadofsky, a founder

Curriculum

The school has no required academic activities, and no academic expectations for completion of one's time at the school. Students are free to spend their time as they wish.

Subtleties of a democratic school

Certain nuances in the operation of Sudbury Valley School emerged during the years it has been in existence, which are essential in defining it:[27]

- o **Political neutrality**

Sudbury Valley School is apolitical. This is a school in which they consciously do not pay attention to the political views of the people who seek to become members of the community: party affiliations, philosophy, class, about any of the features that separate political factions in society. The school does not endorse or support or involve itself with any local projects programs or activities that have a political agenda, while alternative schools and other democratic schools are virtually all identified with specific political movements. The school practices the idea that people of divergent political and social views can work together in a common enterprise where they have common goals other than politics, that political and viewpoint ideas will naturally develop and be discussed by people among themselves, and that the 'law of the land' is fairest and most reasonable when it is pluralistic, and does not formally take sides in aesthetic or political choices.

o **The existence of rules of order**

Official meetings of any group in this school operate according to some set of explicit, formal procedures. The chief function of rules of order is to protect all views and to give them as detached and thorough an airing as possible enabling for decision making, as opposed to the most prevailing models of decision making in schools, the authoritarian model, and the one run as a continuing encounter group, including other democratic schools, which some of them operate without rules of order. Rules constitute the main protection for reason, intellect, objectivity, detachment, and minorities in a group context, as opposed to feeling and emotion. It is the existence of a clear, explicit procedure that protects and encourages people to introduce motions, thence coming to feel that there is access to the political process to all.

o **The rule of law**

The Rule of Law is generally acknowledged to be a cornerstone of orderly, organized society. In this school, laws are always promulgated in writing, and careful records are kept of the body of precedents surrounding each rule. There is a simple process accessible to all members of the community. There is no opening, however small, for arbitrary or capricious authority to step in.[28]

The public schools remain one of the last bastions of autocratic rule in our society. There is in fact no rule of law, by and large the same as in alternative schools where power resides in the momentary whim of the majority at a given instant. They hold the unity of the community to be of prime value and to take precedence over everything else. So they will usually undermine any attempt to institute the rule of law, since that would tend to make an individual feel secure and protect him when he chooses to stand apart.

o **Universal suffrage**

This is the idea that everybody, every member of the school, student and staff, has a vote. It is really a simple idea, as opposed to the idea of democracy as it is sold in Academia, in the heart of our educational system, where the idea is a Greek one: democracy is for the privileged. Confusing the issue of subject matter with the issue of political power.

o **Protecting the Rights of individuals**

This school has a strong tradition that there exist rights belonging to every individual member of the school community, and that these have to be protected in every way possible, for example the right of privacy. Because of this right there is no intervention in the private affairs of students intervention that characterizes other schools, including other democratic schools.

Protecting the rights of individuals is not an absolute concept; it's a much more subtle one where the line is drawn between community interest and private interest that involves a great deal of judgment. The idea of individual rights is absent from schools, because the rights of people in schools other democratic schools included are simply not respected, even if there is occasional lip service paid to this.

Alumni

Sudbury Valley School has published two studies of their alumni over the past forty years. They have learned, among other things, that about 80% of their students have graduated from college[29], and that they have gone on to become successful in many areas of life[30]. There have, as yet, been no formal studies of graduates of other Sudbury schools, but anecdotally, they seem to have similar results.[31][32][33]

See also (online edition)

- o List of Sudbury schools
- o List of democratic schools
- o Democratic education
- o Education reform

References (URLs online)

- o 1. Announcing a New School, [1], Daniel Greenberg, The Sudbury Valley School Press, 1973.
- o 2. The Sudbury Valley School web page, [2].
- ∩ 3. "Sudbury Valley School: About Us". Retrieved 2009-02-28. "Most often students are not concerned about whether learning is taking place. Doing what they choose to do is the common theme; learning is the by-product."
- o 4. Sadofsky, M. (2009) "What it Takes to Create a Democratic School (What Does That Mean Anyway?)". Lecture, International Democratic Education Conference (IDEC 2008), Vancouver, Canada, "Sustainable Democracy: Creating a Stable Culture in a Democratic School." Retrieved January 2, 2010.
- o 5. Gray, Scott D. (1998) "Teachers."
- o 6. Greenberg, D. (1992) "Democracy Must be Experienced to be Learned !" Education in America A View from Sudbury Valley.
- o 7. The Sudbury Valley School, "Underlying Ideas."
- o 8. The Sudbury Valley School (1970), "Law and Order: Foundations of Discipline" The Crisis in American Education An Analysis and a Proposal.(p. 49-55). Accessed 9 Jul 2009.

o 9. Greenberg, D. (1992), Education in America - A View from Sudbury Valley, "'Ethics' is a Course Taught By Life Experience." Retrieved July 24, 2009.

o 10. Greenberg, D. (1987) The Sudbury Valley School Experience "Back to Basics - Moral basics." Retrieved July 24, 2009.

o 11. Feldman, J. (2001) "The Moral Behavior of Children and Adolescents at a Democratic School." Pdf (Explorer). This study examined moral discourse, reflection, and development in a school community with a process similar to that described by Lawrence Kohlberg. Data were drawn from an extensive set of field notes made in an ethnographic study at Sudbury Valley School (an ungraded, democratically structured school in Framingham, MA), where students, ranging in age from 4 to 19, are free to choose their own activities and companions. Vignettes were analyzed using grounded theory approach to qualitative analysis, and themes were developed from an analysis of observations of meetings. Each theme describes a participation level that students assume in the process and that provide opportunities for them to develop and deepen understanding of the balance of personal rights and responsibilities within a community. The study adds to the understanding of education and child development by describing a school that differs significantly in its practice from the wider educational community and by validating Kohlberg's thesis about developing moral reasoning. Retrieved July 24, 2009.

o 12. Greenberg, D. (2000). "21st Century Schools," edited transcript of a talk delivered at the April 2000 International Conference on Learning in the 21st Century.

o 13. Greenberg, D. (1987). Chapter 20, "Evaluation," Free at Last The Sudbury Valley School.

o 14. Greenberg, H. (1987), "The Silent Factor," The Sudbury Valley School Experience.

o 15. Greenberg, H. (1987), "The Art of Doing Nothing," The Sudbury Valley School Experience.

o 16. Mitra, S. (2007) Talks Sugata Mitra shows how kids teach themselves (video 20:59). Can Kids Teach Themselves? Sugata Mitra's "Hole in the Wall" and Minimally Invasive Education (MIE) experiments have shown that, in the absence of supervision or formal teaching, children can teach themselves and each other, if they're motivated by curiosity.

o 17. Greenberg, D. (2009) "The Significance of the Sudbury Valley School Diploma."

o 18. Gray, Scott D. (2005) "Some Facts."

o 19. The Sudbury Valley School Handbook

o 20. The Sudbury Valley School Management Manual

o 21. The Sudbury Valley School The Judicial System. Accessed 10 Aug 2006.

o 22. Scott David Gray: A Few Words on SVS Accessed 10 Aug 2006.

o 23. The Sudbury Valley School Handbook: How the School is Governed.

o 24. Hara Estroff Marano: Psychology Today Magazine: Education: Class Dismissed. May/Jun 2006.

o 25. Greenberg, D. (1987). Chapter 30, "The Staff ," Free at Last – The Sudbury Valley School.

o 26. The Phoenix - Cellars by Starlight, Rock-and-roll dreams - Thundertrain return; John Powhida and the Rudds obsess, Brett Milano, 8 August 2003.

o 27. Greenberg, Daniel. (1987) The Sudbury Valley School Experience, "Subtleties of a Democratic School".

o 28. Gray, Scott D. (2001) "JC Etcetera."

o 29. Greenberg, Daniel; Mimsy Sadofsky (1992). *Legacy of Trust: Life After the Sudbury Valley School Experience.* United States: Sudbury Valley School Press. pp. 242 243. ISBN 1888947047.

o 30. Greenberg, Daniel; Mimsy Sadofsky, Jason Lempka (2005). *The Pursuit of Happiness: The Lives of Sudbury Valley Alumni.* United States: Sudbury Valley School Press. ISBN 188894725X.
o 31. Greenberg, D. (1996) "OUTCOMES." Retrieved on 2009-03-19 (see with Explorer).
o 32. Greenberg, D. and Sadofsky, M. (1992) "Reflections of 'SVS Kids,'" "Legacy of Trust: Life After the Sudbury Valley School Experience."Retrieved on 2009-03-19.
o 33. Greenberg, D. and Sadofsky, M. (1992) "Some Final Thoughts," PART VI, CONCLUDING REMARKS, "Legacy of Trust: Life After the Sudbury Valley School Experience."Retrieved on 2009-03-19.

Additional reading

o *Free at Last,* by Daniel Greenberg, is a book often read as a first acquaintance with the school and its philosophy.

The Sudbury Valley School Press [3] is an active publishing house managed by the Sudbury Valley School from its campus. Their catalog includes dozens of books, videos and audio recordings about the school.

o *Freedom to Learn Blog,* by Peter Gray (psychologist), is a site where Peter Gray, a researcher who has worked extensively studying the alumni of Sudbury Valley, maintains a blog [4] where he discusses education from an ecological perspective.
o Raymond H. Hartjen, *The Preeminent Intelligence - Social IQ (Sudbury model of democratic education).* Social skill development and its relevance to the further refinement of the intellect. Retrieved June 8, 2009. (see with Explorer).

Websites (URLs online)

o Sudbury Valley School official website
o List of Sudbury Schools worldwide
o Documentary including Sudbury Valley School, 2009, 30 minutes, www.teachers.tv

Coordinates: 42°19 28 N 71°27 53 W / 42.32444°N 71.46472°W / 42.32444; -71.46472

A hyperlinked version of this chapter is at http://booksllc.net?q=Sudbury%5FValley%5FSchool

19

SUDBURY SCHOOL

A **Sudbury school** is a school which practices a form of democratic education in which students individually decide what to do with their time, and learn as a by-product of ordinary experience rather than adopting a descriptive educational syllabus or standardized instruction by classes following a prescriptive curriculum. Students have complete responsibility for their own education and the school is run by direct democracy in which students and staff are equals.[1]

The name 'Sudbury' refers to Sudbury Valley School, founded in 1968 in Framingham, Massachusetts, the first school of this type; since 1991, about 40 schools of this type have opened around the world.[2] These schools are not formally associated in any way, but are a loosely connected network that are mutually supportive of each other, operating as independent entities.[1] See here the features that apply to the Sudbury Valley School.

The model differs in some ways from other types of democratic schools and free schools, but there are many similarities:

o **De-emphasis of classes:** There is no curriculum or set of required courses, because there are no courses. Instead learner interest guides things, with students studying what they want to study.[1] There are generally no classrooms, just rooms where people choose to congregate.[3]
o **Age mixing:** students are not separated into age-groups of any kind and are allowed to mix freely, interacting with those younger and older than themselves; free age-mixing is emphasized as a powerful tool for learning and development in all ages.[4]
o **Autonomous democracy:** parents have limited involvement or no involvement in the school administration; Sudbury schools are run by a democratic school meeting where the students and staff participate exclusively and equally. Such meetings are also the sole authority on hiring and firing of staff, unlike most other schools.[5]

Sudbury schools are based on the belief that no kind of curriculum is necessary to prepare a young person for adult life. Instead, these schools emphasize learning as a natural by-product of all human activity.[6]

There are about 40 Sudbury-type schools around the world.[2]

School democracy

All aspects of governing a Sudbury School are determined by the weekly School Meeting, modeled after the traditional New England town meeting.[7] School Meeting passes, amends and repeals school rules, manages the school's budget, and decides on hiring and firing of staff. Each individual present whether student or staff has exactly one vote, and most decisions are made by simple majority[1], with the vote of a child counting as much as an adult.[8]

School rules are normally compiled in a law book, updated repeatedly over time, which forms the school's code of law. Usually, there is a set procedure to handle complaints, and most of the schools follow guidelines that respect the idea of due process of law. There are usually rules requiring an investigation, a hearing, a trial, a sentence, and allowing for an appeal,[9] generally following the philosophy that students face the consequences of their own behavior.[10]

Learning

Sudbury schools are based on the belief that no kind of curriculum is necessary to prepare a young person for adult life. Instead, these schools place emphasis on learning as a natural by-product of all human activity.[6] Learning is self-initiated and self-motivated.[11] They rely on the free exchange of ideas and free conversation and interplay between people, to provide sufficient exposure to any area that may prove relevant and interesting to the individual. Students of all ages mix together; older students learn from younger students as well as vice versa. Students of different ages often mentor each other in social skills.[12] The pervasiveness of play has led to a recurring observation by first-time visitors to a Sudbury school that the students appear to be in perpetual "recess".[6][13]

Implicitly and explicitly, students are given responsibility for their own education, meaning the only person designing what a student will learn is the student themselves or by the way of apprenticeship. As such, Sudbury schools do not compare or rank students the system has no tests, evaluations, or transcripts.[14]

See also (online edition)

- List of Sudbury schools
- Education Otherwise British home schooling charity
- Dartington School British residential educational trust

References (URLs online)

- 1. Ellis, Arthur K. (2004). *Exemplars of curriculum theory*. Eye on Education. ISBN 1930556705.
- 2. Marano, Hara Estroff (May-June 2006). "Class dismissed: it's every modern parent's worst nightmare–a school where kids can play all day. but no one takes the easy way out, and graduates seem to have a head start on the information age. Welcome to Sudbury valley". *Psychology Today* **39** (3): 94(7).
- 3. Peramas, Mary (Winter 2007). "The Sudbury School and Influences of Psychoanalytic Theory on Student-Controlled Education". *Essays in Education* **19**: 119(15).
- 4. Gray, Peter. "Nature's Powerful Tutors; The Educative Functions of Free Play". The National Honor Society in Psychology. Retrieved 2009-07-25.
- 5. Gross, Steven J. (2004). *Promises Kept*. United States: Association for Supervision and Curriculum Development. p. 140. ISBN 087120973X. "Based on this philosophy, the three teachers opened the Red Cedar School, allowing children to decide what they wanted to learn, then they wanted to learn it, and for how long they wanted to engage in it. In addition, the school did not discriminate between play and academic work, making students responsible for their choices. Community was established through a shared governance system in which students and adults considered the school's needs and how to meet them, including hiring decisions and need for revenue. There was also a student and staff council that established codes of behavior and met with students who violated them. Clearly, this kind of student-centered, democratic school endeavor was both bold and innovated. It was also remarkably different from any experiement that I had seen."
- 6. Holzman, Lois (1997). *Schools for Growth: Radical Alternatives To Current Education Models*. United Kingdom: Lawrence Erlbaum. pp. 97 99. ISBN 0805823573.
- 7. "Students revel in free-for-all". *Telegram & Gazette* (Worcester, Massachusetts). 1992-04-19.
- 8. Rowe, Claudia (2002-02-20). "In Woodstock, a nonschool with nonteachers.(Hudson Valley Sudbury School, Woodstock, New York)". *The New York Times*.
- 9. Feldman, Jay (2001), *The Moral Behavior of Children and Adolescents at a Democratic School*, Paper presented at 82nd American Educational Research Association Meeting, Seattle
- 10. Marano, Hara Estroff (2008). *A Nation of Wimps: The High Cost of Invasive Parenting*. Random House. p. 237. ISBN 0767924037.
- 11. Schugurensky, Daniel (2003). "Self-governed, Sudbury Valley School begins in Massachusetts in History of Education: Selected Moments of the 20th Century". *Ontario Institute for Studies in Education, University of Toronto*. Retrieved 2009-08-31.

o 12. Collins, Jeff. "The Sudbury Model of Education". Hudson Valley Sudbury School. Retrieved 2009-02-28. "Age mixing provides a safe environment for students to work on their social skills. Students that are not confident of their social skills can practice them and work to improve them by interacting with other students; whether older, younger or the same age. Students of all ages can look to more mature students or the staff as role models. In Sudbury Schools, it is very common for students to learn from other students. Sometimes the teaching student is older than the learning student, sometimes the teacher is younger than the learner, and sometimes they are the same age."

o 13. Gray, Peter (2008-09-09). "Why We Should Stop Segregating Children by Age: Part I–The Value of Play in the Zone of Proximal Development". Psychology Today. Retrieved 2009-10-25. .

o 14. Wallace, Mike (2001-04-29). "60 Minutes". *CBS News*.

Websites (URLs online)

o Jeff Collins, *The Sudbury Model of Education,* Hudson Valley Sudbury School. Retrieved February 15, 2009.

o Raymond H. Hartjen, *The Preeminent Intelligence - Social IQ (Sudbury model of demo-cratic education).* Social skill development and its relevance to the further refinement of the intellect. Retrieved December 10, 2008. (see with Explorer).

o Sudbury Valley School

o List of Sudbury schools in Sudbury Valley School official website

o Russell L. Ackoff and Daniel Greenberg (2008), *Turning Learning Right Side Up: Putting Education Back on Track (pdf) HTML buy.* Over the past 50 years, virtually everything has changed except education. In this book, two of this generation's most provocative thinkers and practical doers have reimagined education from the ground up. They offer a powerful blueprint for a thriving society of passionate lifelong learners. Retrieved December 10, 2008.

Podcast:

o Russell L. Ackoff (2005), *School Architecture: Doing the Wrong Thing Right* (audio - 58:39 min.) (Sudbury Valley School mentioned: 54:05 min.), Program National Summit on School Design, October 6-8, 2005, American Architecture Foundation. Retrieved December 10, 2008.

A hyperlinked version of this chapter is at http://booksllc.net?q=Sudbury%5Fschool

20

SUMMERHILL SCHOOL

For the school of the same name in Kingswinford, please see Summerhill School (Kingswinford)

Summerhill School

- ○ **Established**: 1921
- ○ **Type**: Independent Boarding School
- ○ **Principal**: Zoë Neill Readhead
- ○ **Founder**: Alexander Sutherland Neill
- ○ **Location**: Westward Ho! Leiston Suffolk IP16 4HY England
- ○ **LEA**: Suffolk
- ○ **Ofsted number**: 124870
- ○ **Staff**: approx 10 teaching, 5 support
- ○ **Students**: 78 students
- ○ **Gender**: Coeducational
- ○ **Ages**: 5 to 18
- ○ **Houses**: San, Cottage, House, Shack, Carriages
- ○ **Publication**: The Orange Peel Magazine

- **Website**: www.summerhillschool.co.uk
- Coordinates: 52° 12 40 N 1° 34 22 E / 52.211222° N 1.572639° E / 52.211222; 1.572639

Summerhill School is an independent British boarding school that was founded in 1921 by Alexander Sutherland Neill with the belief that the school should be made to fit the child, rather than the other way around. It is run as a democratic community; the running of the school is conducted in the school meetings, which anyone, staff or pupil, may attend, and at which everyone has an equal vote. These meetings serve as both a legislative and judicial body. Members of the community are free to do as they please, so long as their actions do not cause any harm to others, according to Neill's principle "Freedom, not Licence." This extends to the freedom for pupils to choose which lessons, if any, they attend.

Historically, the school has been at best tolerated by the British Government, although a recent positive inspection report may indicate that the relationship is now improving.[1]

History

Summerhill School was founded in 1921 in Hellerau near Dresden, Germany by Neill as part of *Neue Schule* ("New School"). However, Neill was dissatisfied with Neue Schule's ethos, and so moved to Sonntagberg in Austria. Due to the hostility of the local people, it moved again in 1923 to Lyme Regis in England. The house in Lyme Regis was called Summerhill, and this became the name of the school. In 1927 it moved to its present site in Leiston, Suffolk, England. It had to move again temporarily to Ffestiniog, Wales, during World War II so that the site could be used as a British Army training camp.[2]

After Neill died in 1973 it was run by his wife, Ena, until 1985.[2]

Today it is a boarding and day school serving primary and secondary education in a democratic fashion. It is now run by Neill's daughter, Zoe Neill Readhead[3].

Although the school's founding could arguably be dated to other years, the school itself marks 1921 as the year of its establishment.[2]

Philosophy

Summerhill is noted for its philosophy that children learn best with freedom from coercion. All lessons are optional, and pupils are free to choose what to do with their time. Neill founded Summerhill with the belief that "the function of a child is to live his own life not the life that his anxious parents think he should live, not a life according to the purpose of an educator who thinks he knows best."[4][5]

In addition to taking control of their own time, pupils can participate in the self-governing community of the school. School meetings are held three times a week, where pupils and staff alike have an equal voice in the decisions that affect their day-to-day lives, discussing issues and creating or changing school laws. The rules agreed at these meetings are wide ranging - from agreeing on acceptable bed times to making nudity allowed at the poolside. Meetings are also an opportunity for the community to vote on a course of action for unresolved conflicts, such as a fine for a theft (usually the fine consists of having to pay back the amount stolen).

In creating its laws and dealing out sanctions, the school meeting generally applies A.S. Neill's maxim "Freedom not Licence" (he wrote a book of the same name); the principle that you can do as you please, so long as it doesn't cause harm to others. Hence, you are free to swear as much as you like, within the school grounds, but calling someone else an offensive name is license.

It is upon these major principles, namely, democracy, equality and freedom that Summerhill School operates.

Conflict Resolution

There are two main methods of resolving conflicts at Summerhill.

Ombudsmen

In the first instance, one should go to an ombudsman to resolve a conflict. The ombudsmen are an elected committee of older members of the community, whose job it is to intervene in disputes. One party will go and find an ombudsman and ask for an "Ombudsman Case". Often, all the ombudsman has to do is warn someone to stop causing a nuisance. Sometimes, if the dispute is more complex, the ombudsman must mediate. If the conflict cannot be resolved there and then, or the ombudsman's warnings are ignored, the case can be brought before the school meeting.

In special cases, the meeting sometimes assigns an individual their own "special ombudsman", an ombudsman who only takes cases from one person. This usually happens if a particular child is being consistently bullied, or has problems with the language (in which case someone who is bi-lingual, in English and the language of the child in question, is chosen as the ombudsman.)

The Tribunal

The tribunal is the school meeting which concerns itself with people who break the school rules. Sometimes there is a separate meeting for the tribunal, and sometimes the legislative and judicial meetings are combined. This is itself a matter which can be decided by the meeting.

A "tribunal case" consists of one person "bringing up" another, or a group of people. The person bringing the case states the problem, the chairperson asks those accused if they did it, and if they have anything to say, then calls for any witnesses. If the accused admits to the offence, or there are reliable witness statements, the chair will call for proposals. Otherwise, the floor is opened to discussion.

If there is no clear evidence as to who is guilty (for instance, in the case of an unobserved theft), an "investigation committee" is often appointed. The investigation committee has the power to search people's rooms or lockers, and to question people. They will bring the case back to the next meeting if they are able to obtain any new evidence. In a community as small as Summerhill, few events go totally unnoticed, and matters are usually resolved quickly.

Once it has been established that a person has broken the rules, the meeting must propose and then vote to decide a fine. For most school rules, there is a "standard fine" mandated for breaking them, somewhat equivalent to a judge's sentencing guidelines, but a different fine can still be proposed. Fines can include a "strong warning" administered by the chair, a monetary fine, loss of privileges (for instance, not being allowed out of school, or being the last to be served lunch) or a "work fine"; picking up litter for a set time or similar job of benefit to the community. In the case of theft, it is usually considered sufficient for the thief to return what was stolen. Although there are some rare cases where the property stolen is no longer in the possession of the thief, in these cases the thief is given one of the two more serious fines and is questioned as to where the property has been sent.

Educational structure

[4]

Although Neill was more concerned with the social development of children than their academic development, Summerhill nevertheless has some important differences in its approach to teaching. There is no concept of a "year" or "form" at Summerhill. Instead, children are placed according to their ability in a given subject. It is not uncommon for a single class to have pupils of widely varying ages, or for pupils as young as 13 or 14 to take GCSE examinations. This structure reflects a belief that children should progress at their own pace, rather than having to meet a set standard by a certain age.

There are also two classrooms which operate on a "drop-in" basis for all or part of the day, the workshop and the art room. Anyone can come to these classrooms and, with supervision, make just about anything. Children commonly play with wooden toys (usually swords or guns) they have made themselves, and much of the furniture and décor in the school has been likewise constructed by students.[6]

Boarding houses and pastoral care

[7]

Children at Summerhill are placed in one of five groups which correspond to the buildings in which they are accommodated. Placement is generally decided at the beginning of term by the Principal, in theory according to age. In practice, a younger child may take priority if they have been waiting a long time for a place, if they have many friends in the upper group or if they show a maturity characteristic of a member of the upper group.

Certain school rules pertain specifically to certain age groups, for instance, no one else may ride a San kid's bicycle, and only Shack and Carriage kids are allowed to build camp fires. The rules concerning when children must go to bed are also made according to age group.

Bedrooms generally accommodate four or five children.

Houseparents

Each of the boarding houses (save the Carriages, see below) has a "houseparent": a member of staff whose duty is pastoral care. The duties of a houseparent include doing their charges' laundry, treating minor injuries and ailments, taking them to the doctor's surgery or hospital for more serious complaints, and general emotional support. Depending on the age group, they might also tell them bedtime stories, keep their valuables secure, escort them into town to spend their pocket money or speak on their behalf in the meetings.

San

Ages 6 8 (approx)

The San building is an outbuilding, near the primary classrooms; its name derives from the fact that it was originally built as a sanitarium. When there proved to be insufficient demand for a separate sanitarium, it was given over to accommodation for the youngest children and their houseparent. At one time, San kids were housed in the main school building, and the San building used as the library. They have since moved back, and the rooms they previously occupied now house the Cottage Kids.

The laws of the school generally protect San kids, both by disallowing them from engaging in certain dangerous activities and preventing older kids from bullying, swindling or otherwise abusing their juniors. San kids have the right to bring up their cases at the beginning of the school meeting or have another student or a teacher bring the issue or issues up on their behalf.

San children can sleep in mixed sex rooms, while older children have single sex rooms.

Cottage

Ages 9 10 (approx)

Cottage kids were originally housed in Neill's old cottage, at the edge of the school grounds. For some time, the San wholly replaced the Cottage, but Cottage kids are now housed in the main school building.

Children at Summerhill around this age (what Neill termed "the gangster age") often begin to "act out", possibly becoming more aggressive or stealing. For this reason, it is advantageous to separate them from the more vulnerable younger children.

House

Ages 11 12 (approx)

House kids are accommodated in the main school building, called simply "the House". They are generally the most unruly and disruptive of Summerhill children (continuing Neill's gangster age), and often practice late-night "sneak outs", or leaving their rooms without permission after lights out.

Shack

Ages 13 14 (approx)

The Shack buildings (there are two, the Boy's Shack and the Girl's Shack) are small outbuildings, so called because of the somewhat ramshackle nature of their original construction. The buildings have since been renovated.

Children of Shack age and above are expected to take a more active role in running the school, standing for committees, chairing the meetings, acting as Ombudsmen to resolve disputes and speaking in the school meetings. Of course, younger children can take on most of these roles if they so wish, and none of them are compulsory even for the older children.

Carriages

Ages 15+ (approx)

The carriage buildings are similar to those of the Shack, only larger. However, they were originally converted rail carriages. Since the last renovation, the Boy's Carriage building incorporates a kitchenette and the Girl's Carriages a common room and shower block (other bathrooms in the school have only baths.) Either facility may be used by both sexes.

The Carriage kids each have individual rooms, and are not looked after by a house-parent. Instead they are expected to do their own laundry and generally look after themselves, although there is a rota for staff members to take care of any Carriage kids who become ill, and they are free to consult the Shack houseparent if they feel in need of adult advice or medical assistance.

Government inspections

Summerhill has had a less than perfect relationship with the British government, and is still the most inspected school in the country. During the 1990s, it was inspected nine times. It later emerged that this was because OFSTED (The "OFfice for STandards in EDucation") had placed Summerhill on a secret 'hit list' of 61 independent schools marked as TBW (To Be Watched).[8]

In March 1999, following a major inspection from OFSTED, the then Secretary of State for Education and Employment, David Blunkett, issued the school with a notice of complaint, which took issue with the school's policy of non-compulsory lessons. Failure to comply with such a notice within six months usually leads to closure; however, Summerhill chose to contest the notice in court.[9]

The case went before a special educational tribunal in March 2000, at which the school was represented by noted human rights lawyer Geoffrey Robertson QC. Four days into the hearing, the government's case collapsed, and a settlement was agreed. The pupils who were attending the hearing that day took over the courtroom and held a school meeting to debate whether to accept the settlement, eventually voting unanimously to do so.[10]

The nature of the settlement was notably broader than could have been decided on the judge's authority alone. The tribunal only had the power to annul the notice of complaint, whereas the settlement made provisions for Summerhill to be inspected using unique criteria in future, to take account of its special educational philosophy.[10]

The first full inspection report since the disputed 1999 report was published in 2007.[1] The 2007 inspection was conducted within the framework set out by the court set-tlement, and was generally positive, even in areas previously criticized by the 1999 report. The school maintains that it has not changed its approach since then. [11]

Summerhill in popular culture

Enid Blyton's *Naughtiest Girl* series (The Naughtiest Girl in the School, The Naugh-tiest Girl Again and The Naughtiest Girl is a Monitor) are set in a fictional school, Whyteleafe, that shares many similarities with Summerhill; the children make the rules and hold meetings to discuss and amend them; teachers do not punish the children, who are tried and punished by their peers in the school meetings.

C S Lewis's book "The Silver Chair", part of the Chronicles of Narnia series, mentions a boarding school called 'Experiment House', and the description of this school somewhat parallels that of Summerhill.

The book *Inspecting The Island* by Hylda Sims was set in the fictional school of Coralford, based on Summerhill.

In the film *Rosemary's Baby* the titular character is seen reading a copy of Neill's book *Summerhill*.

Summerhill at 70, an edition of Channel 4's *Cutting Edge* documentary series, was transmitted on 30 March 1992.[12][13]

A BBC drama written by Alison Hume, produced by Stephen Smallwood and directed by Jon East, set in Summerhill and loosely based on the recent court case was screened on the Children's BBC channel, starting in late January 2008. Much of the show was recorded on location at Summerhill, and used pupils as extras.[14]

Quotations

- o "I would rather Summerhill produced a happy street sweeper than a neurotic Prime Minister." – A.S. Neill [15]
- o "No one is wise enough or good enough to mould the character of any child. What is wrong with our sick, neurotic world is that we have been moulded, and an adult generation that has seen two great wars and seems about to launch a third should not be trusted to mould the character of a rat" – A.S. Neill
- o "What cannot be doubted is that a piece of fascinating and valuable educational research is going on here which it would do all educationists good to see" – Report by Her Majesty's Inspectors of Schools, 1949
- o "I would as soon enroll a child of mine in a brothel as in Summerhill" – Max Rafferty *Summerhill: For and Against*. Hart Publishing. 1970. ISBN 0805510753.

See also (online edition)

- o Free school
- o International Democratic Education Conference - I.D.E.C.
- o Democratic school
- o Kirkdale School, South-East London, UK. Another school that adopted the philosophy of A.S. Neill.
- o Malting House School, a somewhat similar school that operated in the UK from 1924-1929.
- o The Nova Project, Seattle, Washington is a public high school based on the same philosophy.
- o Democratic School of Hadera is a democratic school in Hadera, Israel.
- o Sands School a school based on the same principles as summerhill based in Devon, UK
- o Tamariki School a school based on similar principles as Summerhill based in Christchurch, New Zealand

o Stonesoup School a school based on Summerhill located in Cresent City, Florida USA

References (URLs online)

o 1. "Summerhill Inspector's report" (PDF). OFSTED. 7 November 2007. Retrieved 2008-01-28.
o 2. "Summerhill - Early days". Summerhill. Retrieved 2008-01-28.
o 3. "History". Summerhill School. Retrieved 2008-01-28.
o 4. "home page". Summerhill School. Retrieved 2008-01-28.
o 5. "REPORT OF AN INQUIRY INTO SUMMERHILL SCHOOL - LEISTON, SUFFOLK". Self Managed Learning. 2000. Retrieved 2008-01-28.
o 6. Truswell, Humphrey (1975). *Made In Summerhill*. Hawthorn Books. ISBN 080157322X.
o 7. Appleton, Matthew. *Summerhill School: A Free Range Childhood*. ISBN 1-885580-02-9.
o 8. "Education Bill". Parliament. 22 January 2002. Retrieved 2008-01-28.
o 9. "Summerhill on trial". *BBC News*. 20 March 2000. Retrieved 2008-01-28.
o 10. "Summerhill closure threat lifted". *BBC News* (BBC). 23 March 2000.
o 11. "So, kids, anyone for double physics? (But no worries if you don't fancy it)". The Guardian. 1 October 2007. Retrieved 2008-05-27.
o 12. "Liberal Summerhill tries discipline". *The Times*. 4 June 2006. Retrieved 2008-01-28.
o 13. "'Summerhill at Seventy' Channel-4 documentary film (Zoe Readhead on the Cutting Edge film)". Retrieved 2008-01-29.
o 14. "Summerhill: Inside England's most controversial private school". *The Independent*. 28 January 2008.
o 15. http://www.summerhillschool.co.uk/pages/school_policies.html

Further reading

o Ian Stronach (April 2005). "On Her Majesty s Disservice: HMI and Summerhill School" (PDF). *First International Congress of Qualitative Inquiry, University of Illinois at Urbana-Champaign 4 7 May 2005*.
o Mark Vaughn, ed. *Summerhill and A.S. Neill*. ISBN 0335219136. A compilation of old & new writings from Mark Vaughan, Tim Brighouse, A. S. Neill, Zoë Neill Readhead and Ian Stronach
o Matthew Appleton. *Summerhill School: A Free Range Childhood*. ISBN 1-885580-02-9. A recent first-hand account of life as a member of staff at Summerhill
o A.S. Neill. *Summerhill*. ISBN 0-14-020940-9. a book about the school and its philosophy, by the school's founder
o various authors. *Summerhill: For And Against*. ISBN 0-207-12633-X. A collection of essays, arguing both in favour and against the school's approach
o Jonathan Croall. *Neill of Summerhill: The Permanent Rebel*. ISBN 0-7100-9300-4. This is mainly a biography of Neill but of course has plenty of material about the school and Neill's ideas
o J F Saffange / Peter Lang. *Libres regards sur Summerhill. L'oeuvre pédagogique de A-S Neill*. ISBN 3-261-04017-3.

Websites (URLs online)

General

- o Summerhill School website
- o Summerhill: Education for Democracies
- o Erich Fromm: *Foreword, in: A.S. Neill "Summerhill" (1960)*
- o Web site about Summerhill (in German)
- o Website about Summerhill (CBBC series)

Ofsted

- o Report of an independent inspection (An independent report in response to the 1999 inspection)
- o Campaign site to rescind the Summerhill 1999 Ofsted Report Lots of information about the schools fight for survival
- o 'The Work of Ofsted - Sixth Report of Session 2003 04 House of Commons Education and Skills Committee report on the role of Ofsted
- o Ofsted report from 2007
- o BBC Summerhill closure threat lifted

A hyperlinked version of this chapter is at http://booksllc.net?q=Summerhill%5FSchool

21

TAMARIKI SCHOOL

Tamariki School

- ○ **Motto**: know thyself
- ○ **Type**: State, Co-educational, Primary
- ○ **Year established**: 1966
- ○ **Address**: 86 St Johns Street, Christchurch, New Zealand
- ○ **Coordinates**: 43° 32 48 S 172° 41 22 E / 43.5467° S 172.6895° E / -43.5467; 172.6895Co-ordinates: 43° 32 48 S 172° 41 22 E / 43.5467° S 172.6895° E / -43.5467; 172.6895
- ○ **Principal**: Di Scullin
- ○ **School roll**: 51
- ○ **Socio-economic decile** (10 is highest): 4[1]
- ○ **Ministry of Education Institution no.**: 4143
- ○ **Website**: www.tamariki.school.nz

Online image: School sign

Tamariki is the oldest free school in New Zealand and one of the oldest in the world. It was founded in 1966 by a group of parents and teachers interested in preventative mental health. It is located in the Christchurch suburb of Linwood.

Its name is the M ori word for young children.

Special Character

Mistakes are regarded as important learning information and grading is never done. No adult has the right to demand to see the child s work and such access is always under the child s control. The children also have a very large measure of control over the environment; the adults in the school defer their need for a tidy environment to the child s need to experience cause and effect; to experience why order is desirable.

The school is loosely modelled on Summerhill School.

Originally a private school, owned and operated by the parents, Tamariki integrated into the state system as a Special Character school in 1990.

Notes

- 1. Decile change 2007 to 2008 for state & state integrated schools

Websites (URLs online)

- Official website

A hyperlinked version of this chapter is at http://booksllc.net?q=Tamariki%5FSchool

22

THE BEACH SCHOOL

The Beach School

- The main building
- Location
- 42 Edgewood Avenue Toronto, ON Canada
- Information
- Established: 2003
- Closed: 2008
- Grades: JK-12 (ungraded, ages 4+)
- Campus: urban
- Philosophy: Sudbury
- Governance: School Meeting (democratic, vote by students and staff)
- Website: http://www.thebeachschool.org/

The Beach School was a democratic free school in Toronto based on the Sudbury principles of education; The model had two basic tenets: educational freedom and democratic governance. Small and independent, The Beach School was a community of self-motivated learners aged 4 19 who determine their own curriculum, and each have an equal voice in school governance. Located at 42 Edgewood Ave near Kingston Road and Dundas Street East, the school opened in the fall of 2003 and closed in June 2008 because of a shortage of students. The Beach School was incorporated as a co-operative and at the time of closing was one of two Sudbury schools in Canada; the only one in Ontario.

Philosophy

Modelled after the Sudbury Valley School in Massachusetts which opened in 1968 and has inspired many similar schools worldwide, The Beach School community believes that learning which is initiated and pursued by the learner happens naturally, meaningfully, and enduringly. As such, there is no set curriculum; instead there is individual curiosity and self-initiation direct learning. Beach School students are trusted with their own education and are free to draw from the school s resources as much or as little as they see fit. The Beach School encourages self-evaluation; there are no grades, tests, or assignments unless desired. This educational approach is based on the Sudbury belief that everyone is instinctively curious; therefore when trusted to do so, they will discover independently the knowledge and experiences they need, becoming self-aware and resourceful in the process.

Programming

Students decided for themselves what a meaningful use of their time was. Each day at The Beach School was a unique combination of formal and informal activities, including classes, books, video- and computer-games, unstructured play, meetings, debates, tree-climbing, pillow fort-building, paperwork, and cooking. Some people participated in most of these activities; some spent their whole day on one.

A free drop-in program entitled Parent and Tot operated at the school on Friday mornings from 9:30am 11:30 am for children aged 5 and under and their guardians.

The Beach School had been an annual participant in the Beaches Easter parade and they have hosted an annual school play.

Governance

All members of the school community, both staff and students, were equally responsible for the daily affairs of the school.

School Meeting

Decisions on rules and policies, staffing, use of resources, program opportunities, discipline, budgeting, and other communications were made at the weekly School Meeting, which every student and staff member may attend to debate and vote on current issues.

Judicial Committee

Students and staff took turns serving on the Judicial Committee or JC, a group that met daily to formally review complaints about behaviour, and help those involved find solutions.

Assembly

Parents, staff, and students participated in the operation of the school as automatic members of the school assembly, which meets at least twice a year to discuss issues of overall policy involving school by-laws and finances. People who were not already directly involved in the school could be elected as public assembly members.

Board of Directors

The directors were elected by the Assembly and acted as occasional advisors to the School Meeting.

Tuition

Because the Ontario Ministry of Education does not fund independent schools, The Beach School charged tuition in order to fund the basic operations of the school. The decision on what amount to charge was made each year by the Assembly. The Beach School was recognized by the Children s First Foundation through the Fraser Institute, which provides grants for education to disadvantaged families.

See also (online edition)

- Sudbury model
- Sudbury Valley School
- List of Sudbury schools
- Democratic school
- Education reform
- Free school
- Montessori method

References (URLs online)

- http://www.thebeachschool.org/
- http://www.sudval.org/

Websites (URLs online)

- The Beach School official website
- Sudbury Valley School official website
- List of Sudbury Schools worldwide

- ○ The Ontario Cooperative Association
- ○ The Sudbury Model
- ○ Indigo Sudbury School
- ○ Montessori method
- ○ Waldorf Education
- ○ Free Schooling
- ○ John Taylor Gatto
- ○ The Fraser Institute
- ○ Daniel Greenberg

A hyperlinked version of this chapter is at http://booksllc.net?q=The%5FBeach%5FSchool

23

THE CIRCLE SCHOOL

The Circle School is an Integral school located in Harrisburg, PA and founded in 1984, and is aligned with the Sudbury model. The term Sudbury School means that it is modeled after the Sudbury Valley School in Framingham, Massachusetts. It enrolls pre-kindergarten through high school aged children. The Circle School currently has over 70 students enrolled (a record high) and 5 fulltime staff members. It is the only Sudbury School in Pennsylvania and one of the oldest in the world.

Educational method

The Sudbury Valley model of schooling has two defining characteristics. First, the students are free to spend their time as they choose. During the hours they are in school students can spend their time engaging in any activity they wish (reading, playing video games, climbing trees, conversing, studying, playing trumpet etc.). The only requirements placed on them are that they must follow the rules and that they must do a chore each day (the school has no custodian). There are no grades or evaluations, the idea being that every activity students engage in, they engage in because they wish to do so. The second defining characteristic is that the school's administration is placed principally in the students' hands. All the "day to day" affairs of the school are governed by a democratic body called the School Meeting. There, decisions are made concerning such things as student admissions, creating, repealing or amending a rule, suspensions and expulsions etc. The School Meeting is composed of all students and staff members (teachers) and since the students greatly outnumber the staff members most of the administrative power lies with the students. This model of education receives a great deal of skepticism as it is very different than the other methods of teaching.

History

The Circle School was founded in 1984 by Beth Stone, Jim Rietmulder and Sue Narten. They were soon joined by dee Holland-Vogt. The school was not originally founded as a Sudbury Valley School but as a liberal elementary school intended partially as an alternative for the children of the founders. As the students attending got older The Circle School expanded to an elementary and middle school and finally to a full pre-kindergarten through high school enrollment.

Websites (URLs online)

- o The Circle School's Official website
- o Sudbury Valley School's Official Website

A hyperlinked version of this chapter is at http://booksllc.net?q=The%5FCircle%5FSchool

24

THE GROUP SCHOOL, CAMBRIDGE, MASSACHUSETTS

The Group School was an alternative high school in Cambridge, Massachusetts, U.S., in the 1970s. Operating under democratic-school principles, the Group School was established primarily to serve students from working-class and low-income backgrounds.

In 1977, the school described its educational themes as "internal democracy" and an "emphasis on helping youth develop a sense of working-class identity and pride." Founders believed that traditional educational approaches undermined working-class identity by forcing working-class students "to deny their neighborhood ties" and "to ignore or denigrate the knowledge they have picked up on the street." The school developed curricula aimed at reversing this process, in part through course units on family, immigration, and labor history and courses emphasized working-class youths' "ability to control their own lives and to change their communities."[1] Radical teachers also developed feminist-oriented curricula in concert with female students, in an attempt, as Kathleen Weiler reports, to use "the life experiences of working-class girls to draw out themes of race, class, and gender for critical analysis."[2]

See also (online edition)

Democratic school

Teaching for social justice

Notes

- o 1. Adria Reich and Larry Aaronson, "Neighborhood, Youth and Class: An Introductory High School Course on Ethnic and Class Identity," pamphlet (Cambridge, Mass.: The Group School, 1977).
- o 2. Kathleen Weiler, "Feminist Analyses of Gender and Schooling," in *The Critical Pedagogy Reader*, ed. Antonia Darder, Marta Baltodano, Rodolfo D. Torres (Routledge, 2002), p. 295, n.7.

A hyperlinked version of this chapter is at http://booksllc.net?q=The%5FGroup% 5FSchool%2C%5FCambridge%2C%5FMassachusetts

25

THE HIGHLAND SCHOOL

The Highland School

- ○ Location
- ○ Highland, West Virginia, USA
- ○ Information
- ○ Type: Private, boarding
- ○ Established: 1981
- ○ Founders: Charlotte and Steve Landvoigt
- ○ Campus: Rural, 3 buildings
- ○ Annual tuition: $2,250/day student $12,950/boarding student
- ○ Website: thehighlandschool.org

The Highland School is a democratic school for day and boarding students in Highland, West Virginia, USA. Founded in 1981 by Charlotte and Steve Landvoigt, the Highland School is modeled on the Summerhill School in Suffolk, England. The Highland School's new, as of 2009, boarding component is a unique feature in North American democratic schools allowing students to be a part of a democratic learning environment 24 hours a day as well as engage in international democratic school exchanges.

As the Highland School is a democratic school within the broader theoretical framework of democratic education, there are no required courses. Students are responsible for their own educational choices. Staff provide necessary guidance, mentorship, advice, and teaching when appropriate.

The Highland School has hosted students from all over the world. International students interact with local students from central West Virginia and other areas of the United States.

See also (online edition)

- The Highland School Website
- Democratic education
- List of democratic schools

A hyperlinked version of this chapter is at http://booksllc.net?q=The%5FHighland%5FSchool

26

VILLAGE FREE SCHOOL

The **Village Free School** (VFS) is a private school located in Portland, Oregon, United States. It offers enrollment to students ages 5-18. The educational philosophy at the free school is based upon the idea that if children are given freedom and access to resources they will learn. Children are naturally drawn to skills that will serve them in life, such as reading, problem solving, conflict resolution, critical thinking, and leadership. The students at VFS choose what they want to learn and how they want to spend their time. Free schools have existed in the US for fifty years.

For the 2008/09 school year, the Village Free School plans to enroll 50 students. Admissions are designed so that many ages are represented, and enrollment in each age group is limited. Off-campus learning is encouraged and facilitated by staff at the free school. The school has a new "Open School" program for homeschoolers/unschoolers, so they can spend some time at the school and maintain homeschooling/unschooling as their primary plan.

Families

Parents are integral to the mission of VFS, so the school honors the primary attachments of youth with their families and values the dignity and worth of students, staff, families, and volunteers alike. Many different kinds of families find homes here, and families with nontraditional backgrounds are welcome. The school does its best to support, share, and learn from all the people who come to the Village.

Broader community

VFS shares what they learn about active youth participation and self-determination with educators and advocates around the world. During the summers of 2007 and 2008, students, parents, and staff attended the AERO Conference on Alternative Education in New York. This allowed those from the Village to share what they've learned with other free and democratic schools, offered students hands-on leadership and speaking opportunities, and allowed the school to learn.

Advisers

The school has adult advisers who assist youth with accessing resources, and encourage students to ask questions, explore, and play as their intellectual, social, emotional, and physical health are nurtured. Staff believe that when kids learn the art of problem solving in a holistic way, their skills can be applied to any subject.

Physical space

VFS offers vibrant and interactive spaces to study, play, and share. Students are not coerced into following a schedule dictated by standardized curriculum or testing. However, there is a daily rhythm to help students know when and where opportunities are being offered.

History

The Village Free School started in 2005 after three years of planning by a group of folks who mostly learned about each other from fliers posted at co-ops. Surprisingly, few of these initial school-starters were parents; they were people who wanted to give kids a shot at freedom and democracy, with the hope of creating a natural love for learning.

In 2007/2008, the school hired its first Executive Director, Scott Nine. Scott holds a Masters in Social Work, and was one of the original crew who took on the task of starting an innovative learning place for kids. This same year, the school had students from ages 5-18 for the first time, and met the interesting challenges of serving a wide range of youth in a small community.

Non-profit

The Village Free School is a non-profit, and thus relies upon donations and sponsorships to cover the costs related to running the program. The subsidized tuition starts at about $300 a month, which includes a discount for parents who contribute a small amount of volunteer hours to the school.

Accreditation

The Village Free School has chosen not to seek accreditation through the State of Oregon, as it did not want to be held to any state standards that would interfere with the educational approach. However, the Youth Liberation Project, an opt-in program inside the school, is building a program that will include articulation agreements with local colleges. Since each student's education plan at the school is highly individualized, lack of State accreditation is not seen as a barrier. College is a perfectly reasonable option for those who want to attend, and the school will support those students in their efforts. (The school also supports the efforts of youth who are on different life paths.)

Websites (URLs online)

- Village Free School (official website)

A hyperlinked version of this chapter is at http://booksllc.net?q=Village%5FFree%5FSchool

INDEX

Lightning Source UK Ltd.
Milton Keynes UK
14 February 2011

167479UK00001B/25/P